Golden Rules for Getting Money

The Art of Money Making, Investing & Creating Capital

Compiled by

Mark Guy Valerius Tyson

Copyright

This edition copyright © 2017

MGVT LIMITED

Material selected and arranged by Mark Guy Valerius Tyson

All rights reserved

ISBN-13:
978-1974311453

ISBN-10:
1974311457

MGVT

WWWW.MGVT.CO.UK

INCLUDING THE FOLLOWING BOOKS

THE ART OF MONEY GETTING

HOW TO INVEST MONEY

CREATING CAPITAL

CONTENTS

INTRODUCTION

It is important to note the role of Hereditary Ability when it comes to getting money. Although its role is significantly lessened with the ease of which actors, singers, and the new e-celebs can accumulate vast amounts of money, one should note that a victory is not truly won until it is wisely used. The world will soon forget the celebrities of today in favour of the celebrities of tomorrow and their money will soon disappear down various routes. It is only the ones who know how to use a victory that will have any real impact on the world, and anything worthy of remembrance. Should you wish to give the better chance of wealth to your child that currently escapes you, you would do well to choose a partner based on Hereditary Ability.

Remember, You cannot command success, but you can deserve it.

Man is used in this book in its original definition of Man as in 'Human'. With no reference to either sex. 'He' is sometimes used as well, for the same reason.

God Bless

Mark Guy Valerius Tyson.

THE ART OF MONEY GETTING
Or
GOLDEN RULES FOR MAKING MONEY

By P.T. Barnum

CONTENTS

Those who really desire to attain an independence, have only to set their minds upon it, and adopt the proper means, as they do in regard to any other object which they wish to accomplish, and the thing is easily done. But however easy it may be found to make money, I have no doubt many of my hearers will agree it is the most difficult thing in the world to keep it. The road to wealth is, as Dr. Franklin truly says, "as plain as the road to the mill." It consists simply in expending less than we earn; that seems to be a very simple problem. Mr. Micawber, one of those happy creations of the genial Dickens, puts the case in a strong light when he says that to have annual income of twenty pounds per annum, and spend twenty pounds and sixpence, is to be the most miserable of men; whereas, to have an income of only twenty pounds, and spend but nineteen pounds and sixpence is to be the happiest of mortals. Many of my readers may say, "we understand this: this is economy, and we know economy is wealth; we know we can't eat our cake and keep it also." Yet I beg to say that perhaps more cases of failure arise from mistakes on this point than almost any other. The fact is, many people think they understand economy when they really do not.

True economy is misapprehended, and people go through life without properly comprehending what that principle is. One says, "I have an income of so much, and here is my neighbor who has the same; yet every year he gets something ahead and I fall short; why is it? I know all about economy." He thinks he does, but he does not. There are men who think that economy consists in saving cheese-parings and candle-ends, in cutting off two pence from the laundress' bill and doing all sorts of little, mean,

8

dirty things. Economy is not meanness. The misfortune is, also, that this class of persons let their economy apply in only one direction. They fancy they are so wonderfully economical in saving a half-penny where they ought to spend twopence, that they think they can afford to squander in other directions. A few years ago, before kerosene oil was discovered or thought of, one might stop overnight at almost any farmer's house in the agricultural districts and get a very good supper, but after supper he might attempt to read in the sitting-room, and would find it impossible with the inefficient light of one candle. The hostess, seeing his dilemma, would say: "It is rather difficult to read here evenings; the proverb says 'you must have a ship at sea in order to be able to burn two candles at once;' we never have an extra candle except on extra occasions." These extra occasions occur, perhaps, twice a year. In this way the good woman saves five, six, or ten dollars in that time: but the information which might be derived from having the extra light would, of course, far outweigh a ton of candles.

But the trouble does not end here. Feeling that she is so economical in tallow candies, she thinks she can afford to go frequently to the village and spend twenty or thirty dollars for ribbons and furbelows, many of which are not necessary. This false connote may frequently be seen in men of business, and in those instances it often runs to writing-paper. You find good businessmen who save all the old envelopes and scraps, and would not tear a new sheet of paper, if they could avoid it, for the world. This is all very well; they may in this way save five or ten dollars a year, but being so economical (only in note paper), they think they can afford to waste time; to have expensive parties, and to drive their carriages. This is an illustration of Dr. Franklin's "saving at the spigot and wasting at the bung-hole;" "penny wise and pound foolish." Punch in speaking of this "one idea" class of people says "they are like the man who bought a penny herring for his family's dinner and then hired a coach and four to take it home." I never knew a man to succeed by practising this kind of economy.

True economy consists in always making the income exceed the out-go. Wear the old clothes a little longer if necessary; dispense with the new pair of gloves; mend the old dress: live on plainer food if need be; so that, under all circumstances, unless some unforeseen accident occurs, there will be a margin in favor of the income. A penny here, and a dollar there, placed at interest, goes on accumulating, and in this way the desired result is attained. It requires some training, perhaps, to accomplish this economy, but when once used to it, you will find there is more satisfaction in rational saving than in irrational spending. Here is a recipe which I recommend: I have found it to work an excellent cure for extravagance, and especially for mistaken economy: When you find that you have no surplus at the end of the year, and yet have a good income, I advise you to take a few sheets of paper and form them into a book and mark down every item of expenditure. Post it every day or week in two columns, one headed "necessaries" or even "comforts", and the other headed "luxuries," and you will find that the latter column will be double, treble, and frequently ten times greater than the former. The real comforts of life cost but a small portion of what most of us can earn. Dr. Franklin says "it is the eyes of others and not our own eyes which ruin us. If all the world were blind except myself I should not care for fine clothes or furniture." It is the fear of what Mrs. Grundy may say that keeps the noses of many worthy families to the grindstone. In America many persons like to repeat "we are all free and equal," but it is a great mistake in more senses than one.

That we are born "free and equal" is a glorious truth in one sense, yet we are not all born equally rich, and we never shall be. One may say; "there is a man who has an income of fifty thousand dollars per annum, while I have but one thousand dollars; I knew that fellow when he was poor like myself; now he is rich and thinks he is better than I am; I will show him that I am as good as he is; I will go and buy a horse and buggy; no, I cannot do that, but I will go and hire one and ride this afternoon on the same road that he does, and thus prove to him that I am as good as he is."

My friend, you need not take that trouble; you can easily prove that you are "as good as he is;" you have only to behave as well as he does; but you cannot make anybody believe that you are rich as he is. Besides, if you put on these "airs," add waste your time and spend your money, your poor wife will be obliged to scrub her fingers off at home, and buy her tea two ounces at a time, and everything else in proportion, in order that you may keep up "appearances," and, after all, deceive nobody. On the other hand, Mrs. Smith may say that her next-door neighbor married Johnson for his money, and "everybody says so." She has a nice one-thousand dollar camel's hair shawl, and she will make Smith get her an imitation one, and she will sit in a pew right next to her neighbor in church, in order to prove that she is her equal.

My good woman, you will not get ahead in the world, if your vanity and envy thus take the lead. In this country, where we believe the majority ought to rule, we ignore that principle in regard to fashion, and let a handful of people, calling themselves the aristocracy, run up a false standard of perfection, and in endeavoring to rise to that standard, we constantly keep ourselves poor; all the time digging away for the sake of outside appearances. How much wiser to be a "law unto ourselves" and say, "we will regulate our out-go by our income, and lay up something for a rainy day." People ought to be as sensible on the subject of money-getting as on any other subject. Like causes produces like effects. You cannot accumulate a fortune by taking the road that leads to poverty. It needs no prophet to tell us that those who live fully up to their means, without any thought of a reverse in this life, can never attain a pecuniary independence.

Men and women accustomed to gratify every whim and caprice, will find it hard, at first, to cut down their various unnecessary expenses, and will feel it a great self-denial to live in a smaller house than they have been accustomed to, with less expensive furniture, less company, less costly clothing, fewer servants, a less number of balls, parties, theater-goings, carriage-ridings, pleasure excursions, cigar-smokings, liquor-drinkings, and other extravagances; but, after all, if they will try the plan of laying by a "nest-egg," or, in other words, a small sum of money, at interest or judiciously invested in land, they will be surprised at the pleasure to be derived from constantly adding to their little "pile," as well as from all the economical habits which are engendered by this course.

The old suit of clothes, and the old bonnet and dress, will answer for another season; the Croton or spring water taste better than champagne; a cold bath and a brisk walk will prove more exhilarating than a ride in the finest coach; a social chat, an evening's reading in the family circle, or an hour's play of "hunt the slipper" and "blind man's buff" will be far more pleasant than a fifty or five hundred dollar party, when the reflection on the difference in cost is indulged in by those who begin to know the pleasures of saving. Thousands of men are kept poor, and tens of thousands are made so after they have acquired quite sufficient to support them well through life, in consequence of laying their plans of living on too broad a platform. Some families expend twenty thousand dollars per annum, and some much more, and would scarcely know how to live on less, while others secure more solid enjoyment frequently on a twentieth part of that amount. Prosperity is a more severe ordeal than adversity, especially sudden prosperity. "Easy come, easy go," is an old and true proverb. A spirit of pride and vanity, when permitted to have full sway, is the undying canker-worm which gnaws the very vitals of a man's worldly possessions, let them be small or great, hundreds, or millions. Many persons, as they begin to prosper, immediately expand their ideas and commence expending for luxuries, until in a short time their expenses swallow up their income, and they become ruined in their ridiculous attempts to keep up appearances, and make a "sensation."

I know a gentleman of fortune who says, that when he first began to prosper, his wife would have a new and elegant sofa. "That sofa," he says, "cost me thirty thousand dollars!" When the sofa reached the house, it was found necessary to get chairs to match; then side-boards, carpets and tables "to correspond" with them, and so on through the entire stock of furniture; when at last it was found that the house itself was quite too small and old-fashioned for the furniture, and a new one was built to correspond with the new purchases; "thus," added my friend, "summing up an outlay of thirty thousand dollars, caused by that single sofa, and saddling on me, in the shape of servants, equipage, and the necessary expenses attendant upon keeping up a fine 'establishment,' a yearly outlay of eleven thousand dollars, and a tight pinch at that: whereas, ten years ago, we lived with much more real comfort, because with much less care, on as many hundreds. The truth is," he continued, "that sofa would have brought me to inevitable bankruptcy, had not a most unexampled title to prosperity kept me above it, and had I not checked the natural desire to 'cut a dash'."

The foundation of success in life is good health: that is the substratum fortune; it is also the basis of happiness. A person cannot accumulate a fortune very well when he is sick. He has no ambition; no incentive; no force. Of course, there are those who have bad health and cannot help it: you cannot expect that such persons can accumulate wealth, but there are a great many in poor health who need not be so.

If, then, sound health is the foundation of success and

happiness in life, how important it is that we should study the laws of health, which is but another expression for the laws of nature! The nearer we keep to the laws of nature, the nearer we are to good health, and yet how many persons there are who pay no attention to natural laws, but absolutely transgress them, even against their own natural inclination. We ought to know that the "sin of ignorance" is never winked at in regard to the violation of nature's laws; their infraction always brings the penalty. A child may thrust its finger into the flames without knowing it will burn, and so suffers, repentance, even, will not stop the smart. Many of our ancestors knew very little about the principle of ventilation. They did not know much about oxygen, whatever other "gin" they might have been acquainted with; and consequently they built their houses with little seven-by-nine feet bedrooms, and these good old pious Puritans would lock themselves up in one of these cells, say their prayers and go to bed. In the morning they would devoutly return thanks for the "preservation of their lives," during the night, and nobody had better reason to be thankful. Probably some big crack in the window, or in the door, let in a little fresh air, and thus saved them.

Many persons knowingly violate the laws of nature against their better impulses, for the sake of fashion. For instance, there is one thing that nothing living except a vile worm ever naturally loved, and that is tobacco; yet how many persons there are who deliberately train an unnatural appetite, and overcome this implanted aversion for tobacco, to such a degree that they get to love it. They have got hold of a poisonous, filthy weed, or rather that takes a firm hold of them. Here are married men who run about spitting tobacco juice on the carpet and floors, and sometimes even upon their wives besides. They do not kick their wives out of doors like drunken men, but their wives, I have no doubt, often wish they were outside of the house. Another perilous feature is that this artificial appetite, like jealousy, "grows by what it feeds on;" when you love that which is unnatural, a stronger appetite is created for the hurtful thing than the natural desire for what is harmless. There is an old proverb which says that "habit is second nature," but an artificial habit is stronger than nature. Take for instance, an old tobacco-chewer; his love for the "quid" is stronger than his love for any particular kind of food. He can give up roast beef easier than give up the weed.

Young lads regret that they are not men; they would like to go to bed boys and wake up men; and to accomplish this they copy the bad habits of their seniors. Little Tommy and Johnny see their fathers or uncles smoke a pipe, and they say, "If I could only do that, I would be a man too; uncle John has gone out and left his pipe of tobacco, let us try it." They take a match and light it, and then puff away. "We will learn to smoke; do you like it Johnny?" That lad dolefully replies: "Not very much; it tastes bitter;" by and by he grows pale, but he persists and he soon offers up a sacrifice on the altar of fashion; but the boys stick to it and persevere until at last they conquer their natural appetites and become the victims of acquired tastes.

I speak "by the book," for I have noticed its effects on myself, having gone so far as to smoke ten or fifteen cigars a day; although I have not used the weed during the last fourteen years, and never shall again. The more a man smokes, the more he craves smoking; the last cigar smoked simply excites the desire for another, and so on incessantly.

Take the tobacco-chewer. In the morning, when he gets up, he puts a quid in his mouth and keeps it there all day, never taking it out except to exchange it for a fresh one, or when he is going to eat; oh! yes, at intervals during the day and evening, many a chewer takes out the quid and holds it in his hand long enough to take a drink, and then pop it goes back again. This simply proves that the appetite for rum is even stronger than that for tobacco. When the tobacco-chewer goes to your country seat and you show him your grapery and fruit house, and the beauties of your garden, when you offer him some fresh, ripe fruit, and say, "My friend, I have got here the most delicious apples, and pears, and peaches, and apricots; I have imported them from Spain, France and Italy—just see those luscious grapes; there is nothing more delicious nor more healthy than ripe fruit, so help yourself; I want to see you delight yourself with these things;" he will roll the dear quid under his tongue and answer, "No, I thank you, I have got tobacco in my mouth." His palate has become narcotized by the noxious weed, and he has lost, in a great measure, the delicate and enviable taste for fruits. This shows what expensive, useless and injurious habits men will get into. I speak from experience. I have smoked until I trembled like an aspen leaf, the blood rushed to my head, and I had a palpitation of the heart which I thought was heart disease, till I was almost killed with fright. When I consulted my physician, he said "break off tobacco using." I was not only injuring my health and spending a great deal of money, but I was setting a bad example. I obeyed his counsel. No young man in the world ever looked so beautiful, as he thought he did, behind a fifteen cent cigar or a meerschaum!

These remarks apply with tenfold force to the use of intoxicating drinks. To make money, requires a clear brain. A man has got to see that two and two make four; he must lay all his plans with reflection and forethought, and closely examine all the details and the ins and outs of business. As no man can succeed in business unless he has a brain to enable him to lay his plans, and reason to guide him in their execution, so, no matter how bountifully a man may be blessed with intelligence, if the brain is muddled, and his judgment warped by intoxicating drinks, it is impossible for him to carry on business successfully. How many good opportunities have passed, never to return, while a man was sipping a "social glass," with his friend! How many foolish bargains have been made under the influence of the "nervine," which temporarily makes its victim think he is rich. How many important chances have been put off until to-morrow, and then forever, because the wine cup has thrown the system into a state of lassitude, neutralizing the energies so essential to success in business. Verily, "wine is a mocker." The use of intoxicating drinks as a beverage, is as much an infatuation, as is the smoking of opium by the Chinese, and the former is quite as destructive to the success of the business man as the latter. It is an unmitigated evil, utterly indefensible in the light of philosophy; religion or good sense. It is the parent of nearly every other evil in our country.

DON'T MISTAKE YOUR VOCATION

The safest plan, and the one most sure of success for the young man starting in life, is to select the vocation which is most congenial to his tastes. Parents and guardians are often quite too negligent in regard to this. It very common for a father to say, for example: "I have five boys. I will make Billy a clergyman; John a lawyer; Tom a doctor, and Dick a farmer." He then goes into town and looks about to see what he will do with Sammy. He returns home and says "Sammy, I see watch-making is a nice genteel business; I think I will make you a goldsmith." He does this, regardless of Sam's natural inclinations, or genius.

We are all, no doubt, born for a wise purpose. There is as much diversity in our brains as in our countenances. Some are born natural mechanics, while some have great aversion to machinery. Let a dozen boys of ten years get together, and you will soon observe two or three are "whittling" out some ingenious device; working with locks or complicated machinery. When they were but five years old, their father could find no toy to please them like a puzzle. They are natural mechanics; but the other eight or nine boys have different aptitudes. I belong to the latter class; I never had the slightest love for mechanism; on the contrary, I have a sort of abhorrence for complicated machinery. I never had ingenuity enough to whittle a cider tap so it would not leak. I never could make a pen that I could write with, or understand the principle of a steam engine. If a man was to take such a boy as I was, and attempt to make a watchmaker of him, the boy might, after an apprenticeship of five or seven years, be able to take apart and put together a watch; but all through life he would be working up hill and seizing every excuse for leaving his work and idling away his time. Watchmaking is repulsive to him.

Unless a man enters upon the vocation intended for him by nature, and best suited to his peculiar genius, he cannot succeed. I am glad to believe that the majority of persons do find their right vocation. Yet we see many who have mistaken their calling, from the blacksmith up (or down) to the clergyman. You will see, for instance, that extraordinary linguist the "learned blacksmith," who ought to have been a teacher of languages; and you may have seen lawyers, doctors and clergymen who were better fitted by nature for the anvil or the lapstone.

SELECT THE RIGHT LOCATION

After securing the right vocation, you must be careful to select the proper location. You may have been cut out for a hotel keeper, and they say it requires a genius to "know how to keep a hotel." You might conduct a hotel like clock-work, and provide satisfactorily for five hundred guests every day; yet, if you should locate your house in a small village where there is no railroad communication or public travel, the location would be your ruin. It is equally important that you do not commence business where there are already enough to meet all demands in the same occupation. I remember a case which illustrates this subject. When I was in London in 1858, I was passing down Holborn with an English friend and came to the "penny shows." They had immense cartoons outside, portraying the wonderful curiosities to be seen "all for a penny." Being a little in the "show line" myself, I said "let us go in here." We soon found ourselves in the presence of the illustrious showman, and he proved to be the sharpest man in that line I had ever met. He told us some extraordinary stories in reference to his bearded ladies, his Albinos, and his Armadillos, which we could hardly believe, but thought it "better to believe it than look after the proof." He finally begged to call our attention to some wax statuary, and showed us a lot of the dirtiest and filthiest wax figures imaginable. They looked as if they had not seen water since the Deluge.

"What is there so wonderful about your statuary?" I asked.

"I beg you not to speak so satirically," he replied, "Sir, these are not Madam Tussaud's wax figures, all covered with gilt and tinsel and imitation diamonds, and copied from engravings and photographs. Mine, sir, were taken from life. Whenever you look upon one of those figures, you may consider that you are looking upon the living individual."

Glancing casually at them, I saw one labeled "Henry VIII," and feeling a little curious upon seeing that it looked like Calvin Edson, the living skeleton, I said: "Do you call that 'Henry the Eighth?'" He replied, "Certainly; sir; it was taken from life at Hampton Court, by special order of his majesty; on such a day."

He would have given the hour of the day if I had resisted; I said, "Everybody knows that 'Henry VIII.' was a great stout old king, and that figure is lean and lank; what do you say to that?"

"Why," he replied, "you would be lean and lank yourself if you sat there as long as he has."

There was no resisting such arguments. I said to my English friend, "Let us go out; do not tell him who I am; I show the white feather; he beats me."

He followed us to the door, and seeing the rabble in the street, he called out, "ladies and gentlemen, I beg to draw your attention to the respectable character of my visitors," pointing to us as we walked away. I called upon him a couple of days afterwards; told him who I was, and said:

"My friend, you are an excellent showman, but you have selected a bad location."

He replied, "This is true, sir; I feel that all my talents are thrown away; but what can I do?"

"You can go to America," I replied. "You can give full play to your faculties over there; you will find plenty of elbowroom in America; I will engage you for two years; after that you will be able to go on your own account."

He accepted my offer and remained two years in my New York Museum. He then went to New Orleans and carried on a traveling show business during the summer. To-day he is worth sixty thousand dollars, simply because he selected the right vocation and also secured the proper location. The old proverb says, "Three removes are as bad as a fire," but when a man is in the fire, it matters but little how soon or how often he removes.

AVOID DEBT

Young men starting in life should avoid running into debt. There is scarcely anything that drags a person down like debt. It is a slavish position to get in, yet we find many a young man, hardly out of his "teens," running in debt. He meets a chum and says, "Look at this: I have got trusted for a new suit of clothes." He seems to look upon the clothes as so much given to him; well, it frequently is so, but, if he succeeds in paying and then gets trusted again, he is adopting a habit which will keep him in poverty through life. Debt robs a man of his self-respect, and makes him almost despise himself. Grunting and groaning and working for what he has eaten up or worn out, and now when he is called upon to pay up, he has nothing to show for his money; this is properly termed "working for a dead horse." I do not speak of merchants buying and selling on credit, or of those who buy on credit in order to turn the purchase to a profit. The old Quaker said to his farmer son, "John, never get trusted; but if thee gets trusted for anything, let it be for 'manure,' because that will help thee pay it back again."

Mr. Beecher advised young men to get in debt if they could to a small amount in the purchase of land, in the country districts. "If a young man," he says, "will only get in debt for some land and then get married, these two things will keep him straight, or nothing will." This may be safe to a limited extent, but getting in debt for what you eat and drink and wear is to be avoided. Some families have a foolish habit of getting credit at "the stores," and thus frequently purchase many things which might have been dispensed with.

It is all very well to say; "I have got trusted for sixty days, and if I don't have the money the creditor will think nothing about it." There is no class of people in the world, who have such good memories as creditors. When the sixty days run out, you will have to pay. If you do not pay, you will break your promise, and probably resort to a falsehood. You may make some excuse or get in debt elsewhere to pay it, but that only involves you the deeper.

A good-looking, lazy young fellow, was the apprentice

boy, Horatio. His employer said, "Horatio, did you ever see a snail?" "I—think—I—have," he drawled out. "You must have met him then, for I am sure you never overtook one," said the "boss." Your creditor will meet you or overtake you and say, "Now, my young friend, you agreed to pay me; you have not done it, you must give me your note." You give the note on interest and it commences working against you; "it is a dead horse." The creditor goes to bed at night and wakes up in the morning better off than when he retired to bed, because his interest has increased during the night, but you grow poorer while you are sleeping, for the interest is accumulating against you.

Money is in some respects like fire; it is a very excellent servant but a terrible master. When you have it mastering you; when interest is constantly piling up against you, it will keep you down in the worst kind of slavery. But let money work for you, and you have the most devoted servant in the world. It is no "eye-servant." There is nothing animate or inanimate that will work so faithfully as money when placed at interest, well secured. It works night and day, and in wet or dry weather.

I was born in the blue-law State of Connecticut, where the old Puritans had laws so rigid that it was said, "they fined a man for kissing his wife on Sunday." Yet these rich old Puritans would have thousands of dollars at interest, and on Saturday night would be worth a certain amount; on Sunday they would go to church and perform all the duties of a Christian. On waking up on Monday morning, they would find themselves considerably richer than the Saturday night previous, simply because their money placed at interest had worked faithfully for them all day Sunday, according to law!

Do not let it work against you; if you do there is no chance for success in life so far as money is concerned. John Randolph, the eccentric Virginian, once exclaimed in Congress, "Mr. Speaker, I have discovered the philosopher's stone: pay as you go." This is, indeed, nearer to the philosopher's stone than any alchemist has ever yet arrived.

PERSEVERE

When a man is in the right path, he must persevere. I speak of this because there are some persons who are "born tired;" naturally lazy and possessing no self-reliance and no perseverance. But they can cultivate these qualities, as Davy Crockett said:

"This thing remember, when I am dead: Be sure you are right, then go ahead."

It is this go-aheaditiveness, this determination not to let the "horrors" or the "blues" take possession of you, so as to make you relax your energies in the struggle for independence, which you must cultivate.

How many have almost reached the goal of their ambition, but, losing faith in themselves, have relaxed their energies, and the golden prize has been lost forever.

It is, no doubt, often true, as Shakespeare says:

"There is a tide in the affairs of men, Which, taken at the flood, leads on to fortune."

If you hesitate, some bolder hand will stretch out before you and get the prize. Remember the proverb of Solomon: "He becometh poor that dealeth with a slack hand; but the hand of the diligent maketh rich."

Perseverance is sometimes but another word for self-reliance. Many persons naturally look on the dark side of life, and borrow trouble. They are born so. Then they ask for advice, and they will be governed by one wind and blown by another, and cannot rely upon themselves. Until you can get so that you can rely upon yourself, you need not expect to succeed.

I have known men, personally, who have met with

pecuniary reverses, and absolutely committed suicide, because they thought they could never overcome their misfortune. But I have known others who have met more serious financial difficulties, and have bridged them over by simple perseverance, aided by a firm belief that they were doing justly, and that Providence would "overcome evil with good." You will see this illustrated in any sphere of life.

Take two generals; both understand military tactics, both educated at West Point, if you please, both equally gifted; yet one, having this principle of perseverance, and the other lacking it, the former will succeed in his profession, while the latter will fail. One may hear the cry, "the enemy are coming, and they have got cannon."

"Got cannon?" says the hesitating general.

"Yes."

"Then halt every man."

He wants time to reflect; his hesitation is his ruin; the enemy passes unmolested, or overwhelms him; while on the other hand, the general of pluck, perseverance and self-reliance, goes into battle with a will, and, amid the clash of arms, the booming of cannon, the shrieks of the wounded, and the moans of the dying, you will see this man persevering, going on, cutting and slashing his way through with unwavering determination, inspiring his soldiers to deeds of fortitude, valor, and triumph.

WHATEVER YOU DO, DO IT WITH ALL YOUR MIGHT

Work at it, if necessary, early and late, in season and out of season, not leaving a stone unturned, and never deferring for a single hour that which can be done just as well now. The old proverb is full of truth and meaning,

"Whatever is worth doing at all, is worth doing well." Many a man acquires a fortune by doing his business thoroughly, while his neighbor remains poor for life, because he only half does it. Ambition, energy, industry, perseverance, are indispensable requisites for success in business.

Fortune always favors the brave, and never helps a man who does not help himself. It won't do to spend your time like Mr. Micawber, in waiting for something to "turn up." To such men one of two things usually "turns up:" the poorhouse or the jail; for idleness breeds bad habits, and clothes a man in rags. The poor spendthrift vagabond says to a rich man:

"I have discovered there is enough money in the world for all of us, if it was equally divided; this must be done, and we shall all be happy together."

"But," was the response, "if everybody was like you, it would be spent in two months, and what would you do then?"

"Oh! divide again; keep dividing, of course!"

I was recently reading in a London paper an account of a like philosophic pauper who was kicked out of a cheap boarding-house because he could not pay his bill, but he had a roll of papers sticking out of his coat pocket, which, upon examination, proved to be his plan for paying off the national debt of England without the aid of a penny. People have got to do as Cromwell said: "not only trust in Providence, but keep the powder dry." Do your part of the work, or you cannot succeed. Mahomet, one night, while encamping in the desert, overheard one of his fatigued followers remark: "I will loose my camel, and trust it to God!" "No, no, not so," said the prophet, "tie thy camel, and trust it to God!" Do all you can for yourselves, and then trust to Providence, or luck, or whatever you please to call it, for the rest.

DEPEND UPON YOUR OWN PERSONAL EXERTIONS.

The eye of the employer is often worth more than the hands of a dozen employees. In the nature of things, an agent cannot be so faithful to his employer as to himself. Many who are employers will call to mind instances where the best employees have overlooked important points which could not have escaped their own observation as a proprietor. No man has a right to expect to succeed in life unless he understands his business, and nobody can understand his business thoroughly unless he learns it by personal application and experience. A man may be a manufacturer: he has got to learn the many details of his business personally; he will learn something every day, and he will find he will make mistakes nearly every day. And these very mistakes are helps to him in the way of experiences if he but heeds them. He will be like the Yankee tin-peddler, who, having been cheated as to quality in the purchase of his merchandise, said: "All right, there's a little information to be gained every day; I will never be cheated in that way again." Thus a man buys his experience, and it is the best kind if not purchased at too dear a rate.

I hold that every man should, like Cuvier, the French naturalist, thoroughly know his business. So proficient was he in the study of natural history, that you might bring to him the bone, or even a section of a bone of an animal which he had never seen described, and, reasoning from analogy, he would be able to draw a picture of the object from which the bone had been taken. On one occasion his students attempted to deceive him. They rolled one of their number in a cow skin and put him under the professor's table as a new specimen. When the philosopher came into the room, some of the students asked him what animal it was. Suddenly the animal said "I am the devil and I am going to eat you." It was but natural that Cuvier should desire to classify this creature, and examining it intently, he said:

"Divided hoof; graminivorous! It cannot be done."

He knew that an animal with a split hoof must live upon grass and grain, or other kind of vegetation, and would not be inclined to eat flesh, dead or alive, so he considered himself perfectly safe. The possession of a perfect knowledge of your business is an absolute necessity in order to insure success.

Among the maxims of the elder Rothschild was one, all apparent paradox: "Be cautious and bold." This seems to be a contradiction in terms, but it is not, and there is great wisdom in the maxim. It is, in fact, a condensed statement of what I have already said. It is to say; "you must exercise your caution in laying your plans, but be bold in carrying them out." A man who is all caution, will never dare to take hold and be successful; and a man who is all boldness, is merely reckless, and must eventually fail. A man may go on "'change" and make fifty, or one hundred thousand dollars in speculating in stocks, at a single operation. But if he has simple boldness without caution, it is mere chance, and what he gains to-day he will lose to-morrow. You must have both the caution and the boldness, to insure success.

The Rothschilds have another maxim: "Never have anything to do with an unlucky man or place." That is to say, never have anything to do with a man or place which never succeeds, because, although a man may appear to be honest and intelligent, yet if he tries this or that thing and always fails, it is on account of some fault or infirmity that you may not be able to discover but nevertheless which must exist.

There is no such thing in the world as luck. There never was a man who could go out in the morning and find a purse full of gold in the street to-day, and another to-morrow, and so on, day after day: He may do so once in his life; but so far as mere luck is concerned, he is as liable to lose it as to find it. "Like causes produce like effects." If a man adopts the proper methods to be successful, "luck" will not prevent him. If he does not succeed, there are reasons for it, although, perhaps, he may not be able to see them.

USE THE BEST TOOLS

Men in engaging employees should be careful to get the best. Understand, you cannot have too good tools to work with, and there is no tool you should be so particular about as living tools. If you get a good one, it is better to keep him, than keep changing. He learns something every day; and you are benefited by the experience he acquires. He is worth more to you this year than last, and he is the last man to part with, provided his habits are good, and he continues faithful. If, as he gets more valuable, he demands an exorbitant increase of salary; on the supposition that you can't do without him, let him go. Whenever I have such an employee, I always discharge him; first, to convince him that his place may be supplied, and second, because he is good for nothing if he thinks he is invaluable and cannot be spared.

But I would keep him, if possible, in order to profit from the result of his experience. An important element in an employee is the brain. You can see bills up, "Hands Wanted," but "hands" are not worth a great deal without "heads." Mr. Beecher illustrates this, in this wise:

An employee offers his services by saving, "I have a pair of hands and one of my fingers thinks." "That is very good," says the employer. Another man comes along, and says "he has two fingers that think." "Ah! that is better." But a third calls in and says that "all his fingers and thumbs think." That is better still. Finally another steps in and says, "I have a brain that thinks; I think all over; I am a thinking as well as a working man!" "You are the man I want," says the delighted employer.

Those men who have brains and experience are therefore the most valuable and not to be readily parted with; it is better for them, as well as yourself, to keep them, at reasonable advances in their salaries from time to time.

DON'T GET ABOVE YOUR BUSINESS

Young men after they get through their business training, or apprenticeship, instead of pursuing their avocation and rising in their business, will often lie about doing nothing. They say; "I have learned my business, but I am not going to be a hireling; what is the object of learning my trade or profession, unless I establish myself?'"

"Have you capital to start with?"

"No, but I am going to have it."

"How are you going to get it?"

"I will tell you confidentially; I have a wealthy old aunt, and she will die pretty soon; but if she does not, I expect to find some rich old man who will lend me a few thousands to give me a start. If I only get the money to start with I will do well."

There is no greater mistake than when a young man believes he will succeed with borrowed money. Why? Because every man's experience coincides with that of Mr. Astor, who said, "it was more difficult for him to accumulate his first thousand dollars, than all the succeeding millions that made up his colossal fortune." Money is good for nothing unless you know the value of it by experience. Give a boy twenty thousand dollars and put him in business, and the chances are that he will lose every dollar of it before he is a year older. Like buying a ticket in the lottery; and drawing a prize, it is "easy come, easy go." He does not know the value of it; nothing is worth anything, unless it costs effort. Without self-denial and economy; patience and perseverance, and commencing with capital which you have not earned, you are not sure to succeed in accumulating. Young men, instead of "waiting for dead men's shoes," should be up and doing, for there is no class of persons who are so unaccommodating in regard to dying as these rich old people, and it is fortunate for the expectant heirs that it is so. Nine out of ten of the rich men of our country to-day, started out in life as poor boys, with determined wills, industry, perseverance, economy and good habits. They went on gradually, made their own money and saved it; and this is the best way to acquire a fortune. Stephen Girard started life as a poor cabin boy, and died worth nine million dollars. A.T. Stewart was a poor Irish boy; and he paid taxes on a million and a half dollars of income, per year. John Jacob Astor was a poor farmer boy, and died worth twenty millions. Cornelius Vanderbilt began life rowing a boat from Staten Island to New York; he presented our government with a steamship worth a million of dollars, and died worth fifty million. "There is no royal road to learning," says the proverb, and I may say it is equally true, "there is no royal road to wealth." But I think there is a royal road to both. The road to learning is a royal one; the road that enables the student to expand his intellect and add every day to his stock of knowledge, until, in the pleasant process of intellectual growth, he is able to solve the most profound problems, to count the stars, to analyze every atom of the globe, and to measure the firmament this is a regal highway, and it is the only road worth traveling.

So in regard to wealth. Go on in confidence, study the rules, and above all things, study human nature; for "the proper study of mankind is man," and you will find that while expanding the intellect and the muscles, your enlarged experience will enable you every day to accumulate more and more principal, which will increase itself by interest and otherwise, until you arrive at a state of independence. You will find, as a general thing, that the poor boys get rich and the rich boys get poor. For instance, a rich man at his decease, leaves a large estate to his family. His eldest sons, who have helped him earn his fortune, know by experience the value of money; and they take their inheritance and add to it. The separate portions of the young children are placed at interest, and the little fellows are patted on the head, and told a dozen times a day, "you are rich; you will never have to work, you can always have whatever you wish, for you were born with a golden spoon in your mouth." The young heir soon finds out what that means; he has the finest dresses and playthings; he is crammed with sugar candies and almost "killed with kindness," and he passes from school to school, petted and flattered. He becomes arrogant and self-conceited, abuses his teachers, and carries everything with a high hand. He knows nothing of the real value of money, having never earned any; but he knows all about the "golden spoon" business. At college, he invites his poor fellow-students to his room, where he "wines and dines" them. He is cajoled and caressed, and called a glorious good follow, because he is so lavish of his money. He gives his game suppers, drives his fast horses, invites his chums to fetes and parties, determined to have lots of "good times." He spends the night in frolics and debauchery, and leads off his companions with the familiar song, "we won't go home till morning." He gets them to join him in pulling down signs, taking gates from their hinges and throwing them into back yards and horse-ponds. If the police arrest them, he knocks them down, is taken to the lockup, and joyfully foots the bills.

"Ah! my boys," he cries, "what is the use of being rich, if you can't enjoy yourself?"

He might more truly say, "if you can't make a fool of yourself;" but he is "fast," hates slow things, and doesn't "see it." Young men loaded down with other people's money are almost sure to lose all they inherit, and they acquire all sorts of bad habits which, in the majority of cases, ruin them in health, purse and character. In this country, one generation follows another, and the poor of to-day are rich in the next generation, or the third. Their experience leads them on, and they become rich, and they leave vast riches to their young children. These children, having been reared in luxury, are inexperienced and get poor; and after long experience another generation comes on and gathers up riches again in turn. And thus "history repeats itself," and happy is he who by listening to the experience of others avoids the rocks and shoals on which so many have been wrecked.

"In England, the business makes the man." If a man in that country is a mechanic or working-man, he is not recognized as a gentleman. On the occasion of my first appearance before Queen Victoria, the Duke of Wellington asked me what sphere in life General Tom Thumb's parents were in.

"His father is a carpenter," I replied.

"Oh! I had heard he was a gentleman," was the response of His Grace.

In this Republican country, the man makes the business. No matter whether he is a blacksmith, a shoemaker, a farmer, banker or lawyer, so long as his business is legitimate, he may be a gentleman. So any "legitimate" business is a double blessing it helps the man engaged in it, and also helps others. The Farmer supports his own family, but he also benefits the merchant or mechanic who needs the products of his farm. The tailor not only makes a living by his trade, but he also benefits the farmer, the clergyman and others who cannot make their own clothing. But all these classes often may be gentlemen.

The great ambition should be to excel all others engaged in the same occupation.

The college-student who was about graduating, said to an old lawyer:

"I have not yet decided which profession I will follow. Is your profession full?"

"The basement is much crowded, but there is plenty of room up-stairs," was the witty and truthful reply.

No profession, trade, or calling, is overcrowded in the upper story. Wherever you find the most honest and intelligent merchant or banker, or the best lawyer, the best doctor, the best clergyman, the best shoemaker, carpenter, or anything else, that man is most sought for, and has always enough to do. As a nation, Americans are too superficial—they are striving to get rich quickly, and do not generally do their business as substantially and thoroughly as they should, but whoever excels all others in his own line, if his habits are good and his integrity undoubted, cannot fail to secure abundant patronage, and the wealth that naturally follows. Let your motto then always be "Excelsior," for by living up to it there is no such word as fail.

LEARN SOMETHING USEFUL

Every man should make his son or daughter learn some useful trade or profession, so that in these days of changing fortunes of being rich to-day and poor tomorrow they may have something tangible to fall back upon. This provision might save many persons from misery, who by some unexpected turn of fortune have lost all their means.

LET HOPE PREDOMINATE, BUT BE NOT TOO VISIONARY

Many persons are always kept poor, because they are too visionary. Every project looks to them like certain success, and therefore they keep changing from one business to another, always in hot water, always "under the harrow." The plan of "counting the chickens before they are hatched" is an error of ancient date, but it does not seem to improve by age.

DO NOT SCATTER YOUR POWERS

Engage in one kind of business only, and stick to it faithfully until you succeed, or until your experience shows that you should abandon it. A constant hammering on one nail will generally drive it home at last, so that it can be clinched. When a man's undivided attention is centered on one object, his mind will constantly be suggesting improvements of value, which would escape him if his brain was occupied by a dozen different subjects at once. Many a fortune has slipped through a man's fingers because he was engaged in too many occupations at a time. There is good sense in the old caution against having too many irons in the fire at once.

BE SYSTEMATIC

Men should be systematic in their business. A person who does business by rule, having a time and place for everything, doing his work promptly, will accomplish twice as much and with half the trouble of him who does it carelessly and slipshod. By introducing system into all your transactions, doing one thing at a time, always meeting appointments with punctuality, you find leisure for pastime and recreation; whereas the man who only half does one thing, and then turns to something else, and half does that, will have his business at loose ends, and will never know when his day's work is done, for it never will be done. Of course, there is a limit to all these rules. We must try to preserve the happy medium, for there is such a thing as being too systematic. There are men and women, for instance, who put away things so carefully that they can never find them again. It is too much like the "red tape" formality at Washington, and Mr. Dickens' "Circumlocution Office,"—all theory and no result.

When the "Astor House" was first started in New York city, it was undoubtedly the best hotel in the country. The proprietors had learned a good deal in Europe regarding hotels, and the landlords were proud of the rigid system which pervaded every department of their great establishment. When twelve o'clock at night had arrived, and there were a number of guests around, one of the proprietors would say, "Touch that bell, John;" and in two minutes sixty servants, with a water-bucket in each hand, would present themselves in the hall. "This," said the landlord, addressing his guests, "is our fire-bell; it will show you we are quite safe here; we do everything systematically." This was before the Croton water was introduced into the city. But they sometimes carried their system too far. On one occasion, when the hotel was thronged with guests, one of the waiters was suddenly indisposed, and although there were fifty waiters in the hotel, the landlord thought he must have his full complement, or his "system" would be interfered with. Just before dinner-time, he rushed down stairs and said, "There must be another waiter, I am one waiter short, what can I do?" He happened to see "Boots," the Irishman. "Pat," said he, "wash your hands and face; take that white apron and come into the dining-room in five minutes." Presently Pat appeared as required, and the proprietor said: "Now Pat, you must stand behind these two chairs, and wait on the gentlemen who will occupy them; did you ever act as a waiter?"

"I know all about it, sure, but I never did it."

Like the Irish pilot, on one occasion when the captain, thinking he was considerably out of his course, asked, "Are you certain you understand what you are doing?"

Pat replied, "Sure and I knows every rock in the channel."

That moment, "bang" thumped the vessel against a rock.

"Ah! be-jabers, and that is one of 'em," continued the pilot. But to return to the dining-room. "Pat," said the landlord, "here we do everything systematically. You must first give the gentlemen each a plate of soup, and when they finish that, ask them what they will have next."

Pat replied, "Ah! an' I understand parfectly the vartues of shystem."

Very soon in came the guests. The plates of soup were placed before them. One of Pat's two gentlemen ate his soup; the other did not care for it. He said: "Waiter, take this plate away and bring me some fish." Pat looked at the untasted plate of soup, and remembering the instructions of the landlord in regard to "system," replied: "Not till ye have ate yer supe!"

Of course that was carrying "system" entirely too far.

READ THE NEWSPAPERS

Always take a trustworthy newspaper, and thus keep thoroughly posted in regard to the transactions of the world. He who is without a newspaper is cut off from his species. In these days of telegraphs and steam, many important inventions and improvements in every branch of trade are being made, and he who don't consult the newspapers will soon find himself and his business left out in the cold.

BEWARE OF "OUTSIDE OPERATIONS"

We sometimes see men who have obtained fortunes, suddenly become poor. In many cases, this arises from intemperance, and often from gaming, and other bad habits. Frequently it occurs because a man has been engaged in "outside operations," of some sort. When he gets rich in his legitimate business, he is told of a grand speculation where he can make a score of thousands. He is constantly flattered by his friends, who tell him that he is born lucky, that everything he touches turns into gold. Now if he forgets that his economical habits, his rectitude of conduct and a personal attention to a business which he understood, caused his success in life, he will listen to the siren voices. He says:

"I will put in twenty thousand dollars. I have been lucky, and my good luck will soon bring me back sixty thousand dollars."

A few days elapse and it is discovered he must put in ten thousand dollars more: soon after he is told "it is all right," but certain matters not foreseen, require an advance of twenty thousand dollars more, which will bring him a rich harvest; but before the time comes around to realize, the bubble bursts, he loses all he is possessed of, and then he learns what he ought to have known at the first, that however successful a man may be in his own business, if he turns from that and engages ill a business which he don't understand, he is like Samson when shorn of his locks his strength has departed, and he becomes like other men.

If a man has plenty of money, he ought to invest something in everything that appears to promise success, and that will probably benefit mankind; but let the sums thus invested be moderate in amount, and never let a man foolishly jeopardize a fortune that he has earned in a legitimate way, by investing it in things in which he has had no experience.

DON'T INDORSE WITHOUT SECURITY

I hold that no man ought ever to indorse a note or become security, for any man, be it his father or brother, to a greater extent than he can afford to lose and care nothing about, without taking good security. Here is a man that is worth twenty thousand dollars; he is doing a thriving manufacturing or mercantile trade; you are retired and living on your money; he comes to you and says:

"You are aware that I am worth twenty thousand dollars, and don't owe a dollar; if I had five thousand dollars in cash, I could purchase a particular lot of goods and double my money in a couple of months; will you indorse my note for that amount?"

You reflect that he is worth twenty thousand dollars, and you incur no risk by endorsing his note; you like to accommodate him, and you lend your name without taking the precaution of getting security. Shortly after, he shows you the note with your endorsement canceled, and tells you, probably truly, "that he made the profit that he expected by the operation," you reflect that you have done a good action, and the thought makes you feel happy. By and by, the same thing occurs again and you do it again; you have already fixed the impression in your mind that it is perfectly safe to indorse his notes without security.

But the trouble is, this man is getting money too easily.

He has only to take your note to the bank, get it discounted and take the cash. He gets money for the time being without effort; without inconvenience to himself. Now mark the result. He sees a chance for speculation outside of his business. A temporary investment of only $10,000 is required. It is sure to come back before a note at the bank would be due. He places a note for that amount before you. You sign it almost mechanically. Being firmly convinced that your friend is responsible and trustworthy; you indorse his notes as a "matter of course."

Unfortunately the speculation does not come to a head quite so soon as was expected, and another $10,000 note must be discounted to take up the last one when due. Before this note matures the speculation has proved an utter failure and all the money is lost. Does the loser tell his friend, the endorser, that he has lost half of his fortune? Not at all. He don't even mention that he has speculated at all. But he has got excited; the spirit of speculation has seized him; he sees others making large sums in this way (we seldom hear of the losers), and, like other speculators, he "looks for his money where he loses it." He tries again. endorsing notes has become chronic with you, and at every loss he gets your signature for whatever amount he wants. Finally you discover your friend has lost all of his property and all of yours. You are overwhelmed with astonishment and grief, and you say "it is a hard thing; my friend here has ruined me," but, you should add, "I have also ruined him." If you had said in the first place, "I will accommodate you, but I never indorse without taking ample security," he could not have gone beyond the length of his tether, and he would never have been tempted away from his legitimate business. It is a very dangerous thing, therefore, at any time, to let people get possession of money too easily; it tempts them to hazardous speculations, if nothing more. Solomon truly said "he that hateth suretiship is sure."

So with the young man starting in business; let him

understand the value of money by earning it. When he does understand its value, then grease the wheels a little in helping him to start business, but remember, men who get money with too great facility cannot usually succeed. You must get the first dollars by hard knocks, and at some sacrifice, in order to appreciate the value of those dollars.

ADVERTISE YOUR BUSINESS

We all depend, more or less, upon the public for our support. We all trade with the public—lawyers, doctors, shoemakers, artists, blacksmiths, showmen, opera stagers, railroad presidents, and college professors. Those who deal with the public must be careful that their goods are valuable; that they are genuine, and will give satisfaction. When you get an article which you know is going to please your customers, and that when they have tried it, they will feel they have got their money's worth, then let the fact be known that you have got it. Be careful to advertise it in some shape or other because it is evident that if a man has ever so good an article for sale, and nobody knows it, it will bring him no return. In a country like this, where nearly everybody reads, and where newspapers are issued and circulated in editions of five thousand to two hundred thousand, it would be very unwise if this channel was not taken advantage of to reach the public in advertising. A newspaper goes into the family, and is read by wife and children, as well as the head of the home; hence hundreds and thousands of people may read your advertisement, while you are attending to your routine business. Many, perhaps, read it while you are asleep. The whole philosophy of life is, first "sow," then "reap." That is the way the farmer does; he plants his potatoes and corn, and sows his grain, and then goes about something else, and the time comes when he reaps. But he never reaps first and sows afterwards. This principle applies to all kinds of business, and to nothing more eminently than to advertising. If a man has a genuine article, there is no way in which he can reap more advantageously than by "sowing" to the public in this way. He must, of course, have a really good article, and one which will please his customers; anything spurious will not succeed permanently because the public is wiser than many imagine. Men and women are selfish, and we all prefer purchasing where we can get the most for our money and we try to find out where we can most surely do so.

You may advertise a spurious article, and induce many people to call and buy it once, but they will denounce you as an impostor and swindler, and your business will gradually die out and leave you poor. This is right. Few people can safely depend upon chance custom. You all need to have your customers return and purchase again. A man said to me, "I have tried advertising and did not succeed; yet I have a good article."

I replied, "My friend, there may be exceptions to a general rule. But how do you advertise?"

"I put it in a weekly newspaper three times, and paid a dollar and a half for it." I replied: "Sir, advertising is like learning—'a little is a dangerous thing!'"

A French writer says that "The reader of a newspaper does not see the first mention of an ordinary advertisement; the second insertion he sees, but does not read; the third insertion he reads; the fourth insertion, he looks at the price; the fifth insertion, he speaks of it to his wife; the sixth insertion, he is ready to purchase, and the seventh insertion, he purchases." Your object in advertising is to make the public understand what you have got to sell, and if you have not the pluck to keep advertising, until you have imparted that information, all the money you have spent is lost. You are like the fellow who told the gentleman if he would give him ten cents it would save him a dollar. "How can I help you so much with so small a sum?" asked the gentleman in surprise. "I started out this morning (hiccuped the fellow) with the full determination to get drunk, and I have spent my only dollar to accomplish the object, and it has not quite done it. Ten cents worth more of whiskey would just do it, and in this manner I should save the dollar already expended."

So a man who advertises at all must keep it up until the public know who and what he is, and what his business is, or else the money invested in advertising is lost.

Some men have a peculiar genius for writing a striking advertisement, one that will arrest the attention of the reader at first sight. This fact, of course, gives the advertiser a great advantage. Sometimes a man makes himself popular by an unique sign or a curious display in his window, recently I observed a swing sign extending over the sidewalk in front of a store, on which was the inscription in plain letters,

"DON'T READ THE OTHER SIDE"

Of course I did, and so did everybody else, and I learned that the man had made all independence by first attracting the public to his business in that way and then using his customers well afterwards.

Genin, the hatter, bought the first Jenny Lind ticket at auction for two hundred and twenty-five dollars, because he knew it would be a good advertisement for him. "Who is the bidder?" said the auctioneer, as he knocked down that ticket at Castle Garden. "Genin, the hatter," was the response. Here were thousands of people from the Fifth avenue, and from distant cities in the highest stations in life. "Who is 'Genin,' the hatter?" they exclaimed. They had never heard of him before. The next morning the newspapers and telegraph had circulated the facts from Maine to Texas, and from five to ten millions off people had read that the tickets sold at auction For Jenny Lind's first concert amounted to about twenty thousand dollars, and that a single ticket was sold at two hundred and twenty-five dollars, to "Genin, the hatter." Men throughout the country involuntarily took off their hats to see if they had a "Genin" hat on their heads. At a town in Iowa it was found that in the crowd around the post office, there was one man who had a "Genin" hat, and he showed it in triumph, although it was worn out and not worth two cents. "Why," one man exclaimed, "you have a real 'Genin' hat; what a lucky fellow you are." Another man said, "Hang on to that hat, it will be a valuable heirloom in your family." Still another man in the crowd who seemed to envy the possessor of this good fortune, said, "Come, give us all a chance; put it up at auction!" He did so, and it was sold as a keepsake for nine dollars and fifty cents! What was the consequence to Mr. Genin? He sold ten thousand extra hats per annum, the first six years. Nine-tenths of the purchasers bought of him, probably, out of curiosity, and many of them, finding that he gave them an equivalent for their money, became his regular customers. This novel advertisement first struck their attention, and then, as he made a good article, they came again.

Now I don't say that everybody should advertise as Mr. Genin did. But I say if a man has got goods for sale, and he don't advertise them in some way, the chances are that some day the sheriff will do it for him. Nor do I say that everybody must advertise in a newspaper, or indeed use "printers' ink" at all. On the contrary, although that article is indispensable in the majority of cases, yet doctors and clergymen, and sometimes lawyers and some others, can more effectually reach the public in some other manner. But it is obvious, they must be known in some way, else how could they be supported?

BE POLITE AND KIND TO YOUR CUSTOMERS

Politeness and civility are the best capital ever invested in business. Large stores, gilt signs, flaming advertisements, will all prove unavailing if you or your employees treat your patrons abruptly. The truth is, the more kind and liberal a man is, the more generous will be the patronage bestowed upon him. "Like begets like." The man who gives the greatest amount of goods of a corresponding quality for the least sum (still reserving for himself a profit) will generally succeed best in the long run. This brings us to the golden rule, "As ye would that men should do to you, do ye also to them" and they will do better by you than if you always treated them as if you wanted to get the most you could out of them for the least return. Men who drive sharp bargains with their customers, acting as if they never expected to see them again, will not be mistaken. They will never see them again as customers. People don't like to pay and get kicked also.

One of the ushers in my Museum once told me he intended to whip a man who was in the lecture-room as soon as he came out.

"What for?" I inquired.

"Because he said I was no gentleman," replied the usher.

"Never mind," I replied, "he pays for that, and you will not convince him you are a gentleman by whipping him. I cannot afford to lose a customer. If you whip him, he will never visit the Museum again, and he will induce friends to go with him to other places of amusement instead of this, and thus you see, I should be a serious loser."

"But he insulted me," muttered the usher.

"Exactly," I replied, "and if he owned the Museum, and

you had paid him for the privilege of visiting it, and he had then insulted you, there might be some reason in your resenting it, but in this instance he is the man who pays, while we receive, and you must, therefore, put up with his bad manners."

My usher laughingly remarked, that this was undoubtedly the true policy; but he added that he should not object to an increase of salary if he was expected to be abused in order to promote my interest.

BE CHARITABLE

Of course men should be charitable, because it is a duty and a pleasure. But even as a matter of policy, if you possess no higher incentive, you will find that the liberal man will command patronage, while the sordid, uncharitable miser will be avoided.

Solomon says: "There is that scattereth and yet increaseth; and there is that withholdeth more than meet, but it tendeth to poverty." Of course the only true charity is that which is from the heart.

The best kind of charity is to help those who are willing to help themselves. Promiscuous almsgiving, without inquiring into the worthiness of the applicant, is bad in every sense. But to search out and quietly assist those who are struggling for themselves, is the kind that "scattereth and yet increaseth." But don't fall into the idea that some persons practice, of giving a prayer instead of a potato, and a benediction instead of bread, to the hungry. It is easier to make Christians with full stomachs than empty.

DON'T BLAB

Some men have a foolish habit of telling their business secrets. If they make money they like to tell their neighbors how it was done. Nothing is gained by this, and ofttimes much is lost. Say nothing about your profits, your hopes, your expectations, your intentions. And this should apply to letters as well as to conversation. Goethe makes Mephistophilles say: "Never write a letter nor destroy one." Business men must write letters, but they should be careful what they put in them. If you are losing money, be specially cautious and not tell of it, or you will lose your reputation.

PRESERVE YOUR INTEGRITY

It is more precious than diamonds or rubies. The old miser said to his sons: "Get money; get it honestly if you can, but get money." This advice was not only atrociously wicked, but it was the very essence of stupidity: It was as much as to say, "if you find it difficult to obtain money honestly, you can easily get it dishonestly. Get it in that way." Poor fool! Not to know that the most difficult thing in life is to make money dishonestly! Not to know that our prisons are full of men who attempted to follow this advice; not to understand that no man can be dishonest, without soon being found out, and that when his lack of principle is discovered, nearly every avenue to success is closed against him forever. The public very properly shun all whose integrity is doubted. No matter how polite and pleasant and accommodating a man may be, none of us dare to deal with him if we suspect "false weights and measures." Strict honesty, not only lies at the foundation of all success in life (financially), but in every other respect.

Uncompromising integrity of character is invaluable. It secures to its possessor a peace and joy which cannot be attained without it—which no amount of money, or houses and lands can purchase. A man who is known to be strictly honest, may be ever so poor, but he has the purses of all the community at his disposal—for all know that if he promises to return what he borrows, he will never disappoint them. As a mere matter of selfishness, therefore, if a man had no higher motive for being honest, all will find that the maxim of Dr. Franklin can never fail to be true, that "honesty is the best policy."

To get rich, is not always equivalent to being successful. "There are many rich poor men," while there are many others, honest and devout men and women, who have never possessed so much money as some rich persons squander in a week, but who are nevertheless really richer and happier than any man can ever be while he is a transgressor of the higher laws of his being.

The inordinate love of money, no doubt, may be and is "the root of all evil," but money itself, when properly used, is not only a "handy thing to have in the house," but affords the gratification of blessing our race by enabling its possessor to enlarge the scope of human happiness and human influence. The desire for wealth is nearly universal, and none can say it is not laudable, provided the possessor of it accepts its responsibilities, and uses it as a friend to humanity.

The history of money-getting, which is commerce, is a history of civilization, and wherever trade has flourished most, there, too, have art and science produced the noblest fruits. In fact, as a general thing, money-getters are the benefactors of our race. To them, in a great measure, are we indebted for our institutions of learning and of art, our academies, colleges and churches. It is no argument against the desire for, or the possession of wealth, to say that there are sometimes misers who hoard money only for the sake of hoarding and who have no higher aspiration than to

47

grasp everything which comes within their reach. As we have sometimes hypocrites in religion, and demagogues in politics, so there are occasionally misers among money-getters. These, however, are only exceptions to the general rule. But when, in this country, we find such a nuisance and stumbling block as a miser, we remember with gratitude that in America we have no laws of primogeniture, and that in the due course of nature the time will come when the hoarded dust will be scattered for the benefit of mankind. To all men and women, therefore, do I conscientiously say, make money honestly, and not otherwise, for Shakespeare has truly said, "He that wants money, means, and content, is without three good friends."

PREFACE

The aim of this book is to present in clear form the simple principles of investment, and to afford the reader a working knowledge of the various classes of securities which are available as investments and their relative adaptability to different needs. The book is an outgrowth of the writer's personal experience as an investment banker. Most of the matter which is presented has appeared in the pages of "System" Magazine, through the courtesy of whose editors it is now rearranged and consolidated for publication in book form.

G. G. H.

HOW TO INVEST MONEY

I

GENERAL PRINCIPLES OF INVESTMENT

With the immense increase in wealth in the United States during the last decade and its more general distribution, the problem of investment has assumed correspondingly greater importance. As long as the average business man was an habitual borrower of money and possest no private fortune outside of his interest in his business, he was not greatly concerned with investment problems. The surplus wealth of the country for a long time was in the hands of financial institutions and a few wealthy capitalists. These men, the officers and directors of banks, savings-banks, and insurance companies, and the possessors of hereditary wealth, were thoroughly equipped by training and experience for the solving of investment problems and needed no help in the disposition of the funds under their control. During the last ten years, however, these conditions have been greatly altered. The number of business men to-day in possession of funds in excess of their private wants and business requirements is far greater than it was ten years ago, and is constantly increasing. These men are confronted with a real investment problem.

While they have not always recognized it, the problem which they are called upon to solve is really twofold—it concerns the safeguarding of their private fortune and the wise disposition of their business surplus. They have usually seen the first part of this problem, but not all have succeeded in clearly understanding the second. When the treatment of a man's business surplus is spoken of as an investment problem, it is meant, of course, not his working capital, which should be kept in liquid form for immediate needs, but that portion of his surplus which is set aside for emergencies. It is coming to be a recognized principle that every business enterprise of whatever kind or size should establish a reserve fund. It is felt that the possession of a reserve fund puts the business upon a secure foundation, adds to its financial strength and reputation, and greatly increases its credit and borrowing capacity. The recognition of this fact, combined with the ability to set aside a reserve fund, has brought many men to a consideration of the best way in which to dispose of it. It is obviously a waste of income to have the surplus in bank-accounts; more than that, there would be a constant temptation to use it and to confuse it with working capital. Its best disposition is plainly in some safe interest-bearing security, which can be readily sold, so that it will be available for use if necessity demands.

Confronted with the double problem thus outlined, what measure of success has attended the average business man in its solution?

It is safe to say that the average man has found it easier to make money than to take care of it. Money-making, for him, is the result of successful activity in his own line of business, with which he is thoroughly familiar; while the investment of money is a thing apart from his business, with which he is not familiar, and of which he may have had little practical experience. His failure to invest money wisely is not due to any want of intelligence or of proper care and foresight on his part, as he sometimes seems to believe, but simply because he is ignorant of the principles of a business which differs radically from his own.

The investment of money is a banker's business. When the average man has funds to invest, whether he be a business man or a pure investor, he should consult some experienced and reliable investment banker just as he would consult a doctor or a lawyer if he were in need of medical or legal advice. This book is not intended to take the place of consultation with a banker, but to supplement it.

The advantage of such consultation is shown by the fact that if a man attempts to rely on his own judgment, he is almost certain not to do the best thing, even if his business instinct leads him to avoid those enterprises which are more plainly unpromising or fraudulent. It should be remembered, however, that widows and orphans are not the only ones ensnared by attractive advertisements and the promise of brilliant returns. In most cases, widows' and orphans' funds are protected by conscientious and conservative trustees, and it is the average business man who furnishes the money which is ultimately lost in all propositions which violate the fundamental laws of investment.

The average man is led into these unwise investments through a very natural error of judgment. Accustomed to take reasonable chances and to make large returns in his own business, he fails to detect anything fundamentally wrong in a proposition simply because it promises to pay well. He forgets that the rate of interest on invested money, or pure interest, is very small, and that anything above that can only come as payment for management, as he makes in his own business, or at the sacrifice of some essential factor of safety which will usually lead to disaster.

For the successful investment of money, however, a good deal more is required than the mere ability to select a safe security. That is only one phase of the problem. Scientific investment demands a clear understanding of the fundamental distinctions between different classes of securities and strict adherence to the two cardinal principles, distribution of risk and selection of securities in accordance with real requirements.

One of the most important distinctions is that between promises to pay and equities. Bonds, real-estate mortgages, and loans on collateral represent somebody's promise to pay a certain sum of money at a future date; and if the promise be good and the security ample, the holder of the promise will be paid the money at the time due. On the other hand, equities, such as the capital stocks of banking, railway, and industrial corporations, represent only a certain residuary share in the assets and profits of a working concern, after payment of its obligations and fixt charges. The value of this residuary share may be large or small, may increase or diminish, but in no case can the holder of such a share require any one, least of all the company itself, to redeem the certificate representing his interest at the price he paid for it, nor indeed at any price. If a man buys a $1,000 railroad bond, he knows that the railroad, if solvent, will pay him $1,000 in cash when the bond is due. But if he buys a share of railroad stock, his only chance of getting his money back, if he should wish it, is that some one else will want to buy his share for what he paid for it, or more. In one case he has bought a promise to pay, and in the other an equity.

It is not the intention, from the foregoing, to draw the conclusion that equities under no circumstances are to be regarded as investments, because many of our bank and railroad stocks, and even some of our public-utility and industrial stocks, have attained a stability and permanence of value and possess sufficiently long dividend records to justify their consideration when investments are contemplated; but it is essential that the investor should have a thorough understanding of the distinction involved.

The principle of distribution of risk is a simple one. It involves no more than obedience to the old rule which forbids putting all one's eggs in the same basket. The number of men who carry out this principle with any thoroughness, however, is very small. Proper distribution means not only the division of property among the various forms of investment, as railroad bonds, municipals, mortgages, public-utility bonds, etc., but also the preservation of proper geographical proportions within each form. Adherence to this principle is perhaps not so important for private investors as for institutions. A striking instance of the need for insistence upon its observance in the institutional field was furnished by one of the fire-insurance companies of San Francisco after the earthquake. It appeared that the company's assets were largely invested in San Francisco real estate and in local enterprises generally, where the bulk of its fire risks were concentrated. As a result, the very catastrophe which converted its risks into actual liabilities deprived its assets of all immediate value. This instance serves to show the importance of the principle and the necessity for its observance.

The principle of selection in accordance with real

requirements is more complex. It involves a thorough understanding of the chief points which must be considered in the selection of all investments. These are five in number: (1) Safety of principal and interest, or the assurance of receiving the principal and interest on the dates due; (2) rate of income, or the net return which is realized on the actual amount of money invested; (3) convertibility into cash, or the readiness with which it is possible to realize on the investment; (4) prospect of appreciation in value, or that growth in intrinsic value which tends to advance market price; and (5) stability of market price, or the likelihood of maintaining the integrity of the principal invested.

The five qualities above enumerated are present in different degrees in every investment, and the scientific investor naturally selects those securities which possess in a high degree the qualities upon which he wishes to place emphasis. A large part of the problem of investment lies in the careful selection of securities to meet one's actual requirements. The average investor does not thoroughly understand this point. He does not realize that a high degree of one quality involves a lower degree of other qualities. He may have a general impression that a high rate of income is apt to indicate less assurance of safety, but he rarely applies the same reasoning to other qualities. When he buys securities, he is quite likely to pay for qualities which he does not need. It is very common, for example, when he wishes to make a permanent investment and has no thought of reselling, to find him purchasing securities which possess in a high degree the quality of convertibility. From his point of view, this is pure waste. A high degree of convertibility is only obtained at the sacrifice of some other quality—usually rate of income. If he were to use more care in his selections, he could probably find some other security possessing equal safety, equal stability, and equal promise of appreciation in value, which would yield considerably greater revenue, lacking only ready convertibility. Thus he would satisfy his real requirements and obtain a greater income, at the expense only of a quality which he does not need.

The quality of convertibility divides investors into classes more sharply than any other quality. For some investors convertibility is a matter of small importance; for others it is the paramount consideration. Generally speaking, the private investor does not need to place much emphasis upon the quality of convertibility, at least for the larger part of his estate. On the other hand, for a business surplus, ready convertibility is an absolute necessity, and in order to secure it, something in the way of income must usually be sacrificed.

Again, some investors are so situated that they can insist strongly upon promise of appreciation in value, while others can not afford to do so. Rich men whose income is in excess of their wants, can afford to forego something in the way of yearly return for the sake of a strong prospect of appreciation in value. Such men naturally buy bank and trust-company stocks, whose general characteristic is a small return upon the money invested, but a strong likelihood of appreciation in value. This is owing to the general practise of well-regulated banks to distribute only about half their earnings in dividends and to credit the rest to surplus, thus insuring a steady rise in the book value of the stock. Rich men, again, can afford to take chances with the quality of safety, for the sake of greater income, in a way which poor men should never do. In practise, however, if the writer's observation can be depended upon, it is usually the poor men who take the chances— and lose their money.

In the quality of safety, there is a marked difference between safety of principal and safety of interest. With some investments the principal is much safer than the interest, and vice versa. This can best be illustrated by examples. The bonds of terminal companies, which are guaranteed as to interest, under the terms of a lease, by the railroads which use the terminal, are usually far safer as to interest than as to principal. While the lease lasts, the interest is probably perfectly secure, but when the lease expires and the bonds mature, the railroads may see fit to abandon the terminal and build one elsewhere, if the city has grown in another direction, and the terminal may cease to have any value except as real estate. On the other hand, a new railroad, built in a thinly settled but rapidly growing part of the country, may have difficulty in bad years in meeting its interest charges, and may even go into temporary default, but if the bonds are issued at a low rate per mile and the management of the road is honest and capable, the safety of the principal can scarcely be questioned.

Stability of market price is frequently a consideration of great importance. This quality should never be confused with the quality of safety. Safety means the assurance that the maker of the obligation will pay principal and interest when due; stability of market price means that the investment shall not shrink in quoted value. These are very different things, tho frequently identified in people's minds. An investment may possess assured safety of principal and interest and yet suffer a violent decline in quoted price, owing to a change in general business and financial conditions. In times of continued business prosperity very high rates are demanded for the use of money, because the liquid capital of the country, to a large extent, has been converted into fixt forms, in the development of new mines, the building of new factories and railroads, and in the improvement and extension of existing properties. These high rates have the effect of reducing the price level of investment securities because people having such securities are apt to sell them in order to lend the money so released, thus maintaining the parity between the yields upon free and invested capital.

As an illustration of this tendency, within the last few years New York City 3½-per-cent bonds have declined from 110 to 90, without the slightest suspicion of their safety. Their inherent qualities have changed in no respect except that their prospect of appreciation in quoted price has become decidedly brighter. Their fall in price has been due to two factors, one general and the other special— first, the absorption of liquid capital and consequent rise in interest rates, occasioned by the unprecedented business activity of the country, and, second, to the unfavorable technical position of the bonds, due to an increased supply in the face of a decreased demand.

It will be seen that the question of maintaining the integrity of the money invested is a matter of great importance and deserves to rank as a fifth factor in determining the selection of investments, altho it is not an inherent quality of each investment, but is dependent for its effect upon general conditions. If it is essential to the investor that his security should not shrink in quoted price, his best investment is a real-estate mortgage, which is not quoted and consequently does not fluctate. For the investment of a business surplus, however, where a high degree of convertibility is required, real-estate mortgages will not answer, and the best way to guard against shrinkage is to purchase a short-term security, whose approach to maturity will maintain the price close to par.

The foregoing comments, in a brief and imperfect way, serve to indicate the main points which should be considered in the selection of securities for investment. The considerations advanced will be amplified as occasion demands in the following pages. For the present, the main lesson which it is sought to draw is the necessity that a man should have a thorough understanding of his real requirements before he attempts to make investments. For a private investor to go to a banker and ask him to suggest a security to him without telling him the exact nature of his wants is about as foolish as it would be for a patient to go to a physician and ask him to give him some medicine without telling him the symptoms of the trouble which he wished cured. In neither case can the adviser act intelligently unless he knows what end he is seeking to accomplish.

It is plainly impossible within the limits of a small volume to consider the needs of all classes of investors. Special attention will be paid to the requirements of a business surplus and of the private investor. In the field of private investment two distinct classes can be recognized—those who are dependent upon income from investments and those who are not. Both classes will be considered. For the investment of a business surplus, safety, convertibility, and stability of price are the qualities to be emphasized; for investors dependent upon income, safety and a high return; and for those not dependent upon income, a high return and prospect of appreciation in value. In the following chapters railroad bonds, real-estate mortgages, industrial, public-utility, and municipal bonds and stocks will be considered in turn; their advantages and disadvantages will be analyzed in accordance with the determining qualities above enumerated, and their adaptability to the requirements of a business surplus and of private investment will be discust.

II

RAILROAD MORTGAGE BONDS

A railroad bond is an obligation of a railroad company (usually secured by mortgage upon railroad property) which runs for a certain length of time at a certain rate of interest. It is apparent, from this definition, that the price of a railroad bond, as distinct from its value, is affected by two accidental conditions quite apart from the five determining qualities described in the preceding chapter.

These accidental conditions are the length of time that the bond has to run and the rate of interest that it bears. To understand clearly the influence of these accidental conditions is a matter of the utmost importance. It is evident, for instance, that a 5-per-cent fifty-year bond, based on a given security, will sell at a widely different price from a 3½-per-cent twenty-year bond, based on the same security; yet the only difference is in the accidental conditions which are under the control of the board of directors.

In order to eliminate these accidental features from the situation, it is customary for bond-dealers to classify bonds purely on the basis of their yield, or net income return. As a thorough understanding of this point is essential to an accurate judgment of bond values, whether railroad bonds or otherwise, it must be developed in detail, even at the risk of carrying the reader over familiar ground.

If a bond sells above par, it does not yield its purchaser a net return as great as the rate of interest which the bond bears, for two reasons: first, because the loss in principal, represented by the premium which the purchaser pays, must be distributed over the number of years which the bond has to run, and operates to reduce the rate of interest which the holder receives; and, secondly, because the rate is paid only on the par value of the bond instead of on the actual money invested. Thus, if a 6-percent bond with eight years to run sells at 110¾, it will yield only 4.40 per cent, which means that if the holder spends more than $48.73 (4.40 per cent of $1,107.50) out of the $60 which he receives annually, he is spending the excess out of principal, and not out of income. Conversely, if a bond sells below par, it yields more than the rate of interest which the bond bears.

These yields have been calculated with the utmost exactness for all bonds paying from 2 per cent to 7 per cent and running from six months to one hundred years, so that it is only necessary to turn to the tables to discover what will be the net return upon a given bond at a given price. This net return is generally known as the "basis," and bonds are spoken of as selling upon a 3.80 per cent basis or a 4.65 per cent basis or whatever the figure may be, with no reference whatever to the price or to the rate of interest which the bond bears. Indeed, so exclusively is the basis considered by bond-dealers that very often bonds are bought and sold upon a basis price, and the actual figures at which the bonds change hands are not determined until after the transaction is concluded.

It is not expected, of course, that the average business man will purchase bonds in quite as scientific a way as this, but it is essential that he should understand that while the intrinsic value of a bond is determined only by the five general factors described, its money value, or price, is affected also by these two accidental conditions. Exprest in other words, he must realize that the general factor described as rate of income does not mean the coupon rate of interest which the bond bears, but the scientific "basis," derived by elimination of the accidental features.

Within the past year there has been a good deal of uninformed comment about the safety of railroad bonds. Before the era of popular agitation and governmental antagonism, railroad bonds enjoyed a large measure of public confidence; but it can not be denied that some part of this confidence has been shaken as a result of the recent exposures. Even clearheaded men have exaggerated the importance of the developments; and too often railroad officials, who should have insisted upon the soundness and stability of their properties, when they elected to talk for publication, have given way instead to dismal and unwarranted forebodings.

There is no mystery involved in determining the safety of railroad bonds. Any man of business experience, keeping in mind the general principle which measures the value of all obligations, can easily determine, with the aid of two documents, the degree of safety which attaches to any particular railroad bond. The general principle to be observed is that the safety of any obligation depends upon the margin of security in excess of the amount of the loan; and the two documents to be consulted are the mortgage or trust indenture securing the bonds, which describes the property mortgaged, and the last annual report of the railroad, which shows its financial condition.

Confining the analysis, for the present, to mortgage bonds upon the general mileage of a railroad, the following points should be considered:

(1) Rate per mile at which the bond is issued. Applying the general principle indicated above, it must be learned what proportion the bonded debt of a railroad bears to the total market value of the property. It is much easier to make this comparison on a per-mile basis. In determining whether the rate per mile is excessive, reference must be made not so much to the particular bond in question as to the total bonded debt per mile of the railroad, and to the relation which that figure bears to the total market value of the property per mile. The total market value per mile is obtained by adding the market value of the stock per mile to the par value of the bonded debt per mile. A single issue of bonds varies all the way from $5,000 to $100,000 per mile, according to the location of the railroad. Total capitalization per mile—stocks and bonds at par—varies in about the same proportion, from $35,000 to $300,000. The average for all the railroads of the United States is $67,936 per mile. The actual cost of the railroad, as shown by the balance-sheet, must be taken into consideration, and also the estimated cost of duplicating the property. Physical difficulties of construction must be weighed, for a railroad through a flat, sandy country should not be bonded for as much, other things being equal, as a railroad through a mountainous country, where much cutting, filling, and bridging are required. The section of country in which the railroad is located must be considered, for $35,000 per mile on a single-track line in a poor country may be higher than $300,000 per mile on a four-track trunk line which owns valuable terminals and rights of way through several large cities.

(2) Amount of prior lien bonds outstanding per mile.

The amount of bonds which come ahead of the bond in question on the same mileage is a matter of great importance and works directly against the security of the bond. Purchasing a bond which is preceded by a prior line bond is like taking a real-estate mortgage on property already encumbered. If the bond is not followed by other bonds, then the margin of security in the property is represented wholly by the market value of the stock per mile, and the investor must figure carefully the value of this equity.

(3) Amount of junior lien bonds outstanding per mile. The amount of bonds which come after the bond in question, on the other hand, works directly in favor of the bond, for it increases the margin of security. It shows also that other people have had sufficient confidence in the property to invest their money in obligations subject to the one in question. In the event of a receivership this is often a matter of great importance; for if a foreclosure sale is ordered the junior bondholders, in order to protect their own interest, must buy in the property for an amount at least equal to the par value of the prior lien bonds.

The foregoing considerations apply particularly to the safety of the principal invested in railroad bonds; the following points affect the safety of interest:

(4) Gross earnings per mile. The gross earnings of a railroad must be compared with those of other roads occupying the same field, and the returns for a number of years must be examined to determine whether such earnings have increased or decreased. The position in which the railroad stands for obtaining new traffic must be noted. This is dependent somewhat upon the railroad's ability to take traffic from other railroads, but more upon the probable growth and development of the territory which the railroad serves, and the increased traffic which will probably be offered. In this connection the rate of increase in population in the road's territory is important. The proportion between passenger and freight earnings,

the diversity and density of freight traffic, and passenger and freight rates should be examined. The reputation of the management for ability and integrity should be considered. Gross earnings run from about $3,000 to $40,000 per mile with the average $10,460.

(5) Net income per mile. Net income is obtained by subtracting from gross earnings operating expenses (and sometimes taxes) and adding to the net earnings so obtained whatever income from other sources the railroad may derive. This is a very important figure. As with gross earnings, the reports should be examined to determine whether net income is on the increase or the decrease, and it should be compared with the net income of other railroads occupying the same field. It involves a criticism of operating expenses. The payments of the railroad must be analyzed to determine whether the proper sums have been expended for maintenance of way, replenishment of rolling stock, and other improvements sufficient to keep the road in good physical condition. Normally speaking, operating expenses should absorb about 65 per cent of gross earnings. If it is found that a railroad operates for 60 per cent, however, it does not always follow that its operating officials are exceptionally efficient, so that the cost of conducting transportation is relatively small; it may mean that the physical condition of the property is being neglected, or that ordinary improvements, which should be charged to maintenance, are being paid for by increase in capitalization. It is very important for the investor to find out which is the case. If analysis leads to the suspicion that the earnings result from neglecting the property or capitalizing every trivial improvement, the railroad's bonds should be rejected. Net income varies from $1,500 to $12,000 per mile, with an average of $4,702.

(6) Fixt charges per mile. The fixt charges of a railroad include interest on its bonds, rentals, and taxes (when the last-named are not reported with operating expenses). The importance of this figure lies in its relation to net income.

If a railroad does not earn well over double its fixt charges, its obligations can not be regarded as in the first investment rank. Of course, when a railroad earns more than twice the interest requirement upon its entire bonded debt, it is probable that some of the underlying bonds are protected by three, four, or five times the interest requirement upon them, and their position is correspondingly strengthened.

The foregoing analysis applies particularly to mortgage bonds upon the general mileage of a railroad and not to such special issues as collateral trust, terminal, bridge, or guaranteed bonds. It will not be necessary, however, to lay down any rules as to these classes of bonds, for the general principles outlined above, with slight modifications of detail, will be found equally applicable to a judgment of their value. Equipment bonds, on the other hand, owing to their want of similarity to any other railroad issues, will receive separate treatment later.

It is of interest, in view of the present diminished confidence in railroad securities, to advance certain considerations touching upon the safety of railroad bonds in general.

The last published report of the Inter-State Commerce Commission, year 1906, furnishes interesting testimony on this subject. A table on page 60 shows that the total railroad capital of the United States for that year was $14,570,421,478, of which $7,766,661,385, or 53.31 per cent, was in the form of bonded debt, and the rest in capital stock.

These figures indicate a substantial equity, but are somewhat misleading because they refer to par value. A fair estimate of the market value of this stock equity, which is the margin of security in the properties from the bondholder's point of view, can be obtained from a table on page 82, which shows a balance available for dividends, after paying all operating expenses and fixt charges, of all the railroads of the United States for the year ended June

30, 1906, of $457,060,326. This amount is equivalent to nearly 7 per cent upon the total par value of the stocks.

Estimating that a railroad stock should earn 10 per cent upon its market price—and even the most prejudiced will admit that a stock earning 10 per cent is worth par—the total market value of American railroad stocks would be $4,570,603,260, or more than half the par value of the bonds. In other words, the bonded debt would represent something less than 63 per cent of the total market value of the property. This compares favorably with the security of first mortgages upon real estate.

When the safety of interest is considered, the showing made is equally strong. Page 82 of the report above quoted shows that the net income of the railroads of the United States for the year ended June 30, 1906, after payment of all operating expenses, was $848,836,771, and the total fixt charges, including interest on bonds, interest on current liabilities, and taxes, amounted to $391,776,445, leaving a balance available for dividends of $457,060,326. It is apparent, therefore, that the net earnings of the railroads of the United States, considered as one system, could be cut in half without affecting the payment of interest upon the railroad's obligations. This affords a large measure of protection.

The following analysis shows that the actual market value of the railroads is probably greater than the estimate made above.

The table shows the percentage of bonded debt to total market value of some of the more important railroad systems. Two trunk lines in the East, a north and south line in the middle West, and two transcontinental have been chosen. No attempt has been made to select railroads which would make a favorable showing. Indeed Pennsylvania, and Union Pacific, by reason of their recent heavy bond issues, probably compare unfavorably with others which might have been chosen. The figures showing the par value of bonds outstanding have been taken from last annual reports, with additions made for recent issues. The figures showing the market value of stocks are based on the amounts outstanding April 1st, 1908, at the market price.

Par value of bonds outstanding value of stock outstanding bonds to total value	Approx. market Per cent of	
Pennsylvania	$270,974,645	$361,000,000	42.8
New York Central	255,414,845	174,000,000	59.4
Illinois Central	156,053,275	120,000,000	56.6
Great Northern	207,517,939	260,000,000	44.3
Union Pacific	274,827,000	324,000,000	45.9

In view of the enormous decline which has occurred in railroad stocks during the past eighteen months, the showing above is truly remarkable. It is plain that the entire bonded debt of any of these standard railroads is less than 60 per cent of the total market value of the property, while in the cases of the Pennsylvania, Great Northern, and Union Pacific, more than half of the present market value of the property could be erased before the lien of the bonds least well secured would be impaired.

Of course, where the entire bonded debt is protected by such a margin, it is evident that the underlying bonds (the prior liens and first mortgages) are protected by several times as great a margin and their position is correspondingly strengthened.

The foregoing analysis, in the judgment of the writer, affords convincing proof not only that the prevailing want of confidence in railroad obligations is without foundation, but that railroad bonds compare favorably in point of safety with any other form of investment.

It remains to point out the amount of income and degree of convertibility which they afford and the extent of appreciation in value which they promise. It is impossible to do more than indicate the general characteristics of railroad bonds in these particulars.

Railroad bonds cover a wide range of income return. They yield all the way from $3\frac{3}{4}$ per cent to 9 per cent, the general average being from 4 per cent to 6 per cent. As a class they yield more than government or municipal bonds, and less than public-utility or industrial bonds. With equal security they probably yield less than real-estate mortgages. Compared with stocks they return more than bank stocks, average about the same as railroad stocks, and yield less than public-utility, industrial, or mining stocks. These comparisons are intended to apply to the classes as a whole, and remain generally true in spite of specific cases to the contrary.

Convertibility is the distinguishing mark of railroad bonds. Generally speaking they may be more easily marketed than any other class of bonds. Compared with stocks they exceed public-utility, mining, and bank stocks in point of convertibility, and yield only to railroad stocks. It is hard to say whether or not they possess greater convertibility than industrial stocks, but it is probable that they do, allowing for the fact that an undue impression is created by the activity of certain prominent shares.

Railroad bonds as a class possess great promise of appreciation in value. American railroads, generally speaking, have adopted the conservative policy of putting a considerable part of their annual earnings back into the property in the form of improvements. To the extent to which this policy is followed, an equity is created back of the bonds which raises their intrinsic value. This policy contrasts favorably with the general practise of English roads to pay out all their earnings in dividends, and to capitalize their improvements. In addition, new capital for

American railroads is largely raised by stock issues, which further increases the margin of security for the bondholders. Taken together these facts insure a steady enhancement in the intrinsic value of railroad bonds, which is bound to be reflected, other things being equal, in higher prices.

We shall not attempt to discuss at this time the degree of stability of market price which railroad bonds enjoy. As explained in the first chapter, stability of market price is dependent upon general financial and business conditions. It is sufficient to point out here that the maintenance intact of the principal sum invested can only be rendered certain by the purchase of short-time securities whose near approach to maturity will keep their price close to par. In a later chapter the general principles which determine this question will be elucidated.

The ideal investment may be defined as one combining ample security of principal and interest, a good rate of income, ready convertibility into cash, and reasonable promise of appreciation in value. Measured by the requirements of this definition, the conclusion seems justified that well-selected railroad bonds, if purchased under favorable money-market conditions, afford a highly desirable form of investment.

III

RAILROAD EQUIPMENT BONDS

As its name implies, an equipment bond is one issued by a railroad to provide funds with which to pay for new rolling stock—cars and locomotives. The issues are variously described as car trust certificates, equipment bonds, or equipment notes. They conform in general to one of two standard forms: (1) The conditional sale plan: In accordance with specifications furnished by the railroad, the trustee selected (usually a trust company) contracts with the builders for the purchase of the equipment. From

10 to 20 per cent of the cost of the equipment is paid in cash by the railroad and the rest is represented by the equipment bonds. The bonds are the direct obligation of the railroad company. They are secured by a first lien upon the entire equipment purchased. The title to the equipment remains in the trustee for the benefit of the bondholders until the last bond has been paid, so that under no circumstances can the general mortgages of the railroad attach as a first lien on the equipment ahead of the car trust obligations. After the final payment, the trustee assigns title to the railroad company, which thereupon becomes the owner in fee of the equipment. Under the terms of the deed of trust the railroad is always obliged to keep the equipment fully insured, in good order and complete repair, and to replace any equipment which may become worn out, lost, or destroyed. The bonds are usually issued in coupon form, $1,000 each, bearing semiannual interest, with provision for registration. They are generally paid off in semiannual or annual instalments of substantially equal amounts, the last instalment usually falling due in ten years, a period well within the life of the equipment as estimated under the master car builder's rules. Occasionally this method of payment is altered by the substitution of a sinking fund, the bonds having a uniform fixt maturity, but subject to the operation of a sinking fund which is sufficient to retire the entire issue well within the life of the equipment. In either case the security, ample at the outset, increases proportionally with the reduction in obligations outstanding against it.

(2) The so-called "Philadelphia plan." Under this plan the equipment is purchased by an individual, association, or corporation which leases the equipment to the railroad for a term of years at a rental equivalent to the interest and maturing instalments of the bonds. The contract of lease is then assigned to a trust company as trustee, which thereupon issues its certificates in substantially the form described in the plan above, these representing a beneficial

interest in the equipment, which are usually guaranteed both principal and interest by the railroad. The lease runs until the last bond has been paid, after which the trustee assigns title to the railroad as above. The chief advantage of this plan over the other is that in some States, notably Pennsylvania, certificates issued in accordance with its terms are exempt from taxation, whereas under the conditional sale plan, as the direct obligation of the railroad, the bonds would be taxable.

It is evident from the foregoing description that equipment bonds differ in two important respects from all other classes of railroad issues. First, the title to the property which secures the bonds does not vest in the railroad; and, secondly, the property is movable and not fixt in any one locality.

By virtue of these two points, the holders of equipment bonds possess a great advantage over the holders of mortgage bonds in the event of a railroad's becoming bankrupt.

If a railroad is unable to meet its interest charges, the mortgage bondholders can rarely do better than have a receiver appointed who will operate the railroad in their interest; but if, with honest and efficient management, the railroad can not be made to earn its interest charges, the mortgage bondholders usually have to consent to the scaling of their bonds to a point where the railroad can operate upon a paying basis.

With the holders of equipment bonds the case is quite different. If the receiver defaults upon their bonds they have only to direct the trustee to enter upon possession of the equipment and sell it or lease it to some other railroad. The knowledge that they possess this power renders its exercise generally unnecessary. The equipment of a railroad is essential to its operation. It is the tool with which the railroad handles its business. If the receiver were deprived of the equipment it would be impossible for him to operate the road, and so he could never satisfy its creditors. Consequently the courts, both State and Federal, have ruled that the necessary equipment of a bankrupt railroad must be preserved, and have placed the charges for principal and interest of equipment obligations upon an equality with charges for wages, materials, and other operating expenses, and in priority to interest of even first-mortgage bonds.

These points sufficiently explain the remarkable record which equipment bonds have made during reorganizations. Careful investigation has been made of the various railroads which were reorganized, either with or without foreclosure, between the years 1888 and 1905. This covers the chief period of railroad receivership. It was discovered that sixteen different railroads, aggregating nearly one hundred thousand miles and located in widely different parts of the country, had outstanding equipment bonds at the time of default. In every case the principal and interest of equipment bonds were paid in full, while all other securities, with a few exceptions, were reduced in rate or amount or both. Two of these railroads offered to the holders of equipment bonds the option of an advantageous exchange of securities, which amounted to more than payment in full.

The foregoing facts justify the conclusion that equipment bonds possess security equal or superior to that of any other form of railroad bonds.

Let us now consider their remaining characteristics— their rate of income, convertibility, prospect of appreciation in value, and stability of market price.

One of the strongest features of equipment bonds is the relatively high rate of income which they yield. The amount realized varies in accordance with the financial strength and credit of the issuing railroad, and the margin of security in the equipment itself. As a general rule, the net return on the equipment bonds of a given railroad is usually from ½ per cent to ¾ per cent greater than on the first-mortgage bonds of the same railroad. This is owing to the fact that while banks and scientific investors have bought equipment bonds for many years, the general public is not sufficiently familiar with the inherent strength of these issues to create much of a demand for them. This insures a good return.

Equipment bonds vary in point of convertibility. The reader will remember from the description above that equipment bonds are usually issued in serial form, with instalments maturing semiannually from six months to ten years. By confining purchases to the shorter maturities, say within two or three years, a high degree of convertibility may usually be obtained because the short maturities are greatly sought by banks and other financial institutions which regard equipment bonds in much the same light as merchant's paper or time loans secured by collateral. At a price equivalent to the rate which the best commercial paper commands, there is always a good demand from the banks. Many banks prefer equipment bonds to loans or paper on account of their greater convertibility. As the length of maturity increases, the degree of convertibility generally decreases, because the chief demand for the longer dates comes from insurance companies, which do not, in the aggregate, constitute as great a demand as the banks. When the demand from private investors increases, as it undoubtedly will when they become more familiar with the desirable points of these issues, all maturities will probably possess ready convertibility.

In the same way, equipment bonds vary as to stability of market price. Compared with other classes of railroad issues, equipment bonds are all relatively stable, but the stability is especially marked in the shorter maturities.

Equipment bonds possess little prospect of appreciation in value.

The attentive reader who has carefully followed the foregoing description of equipment bonds, may have noticed a special adaptability on their part to the requirements of a business surplus. Broadly speaking, for such investment, a security is required which will combine perfect safety of principal and interest, a good rate of income, ready convertibility into cash, and unyielding stability of market price. The necessity for insistence upon these requirements in the investment of a business surplus will appear upon a moment's reflection. Safety is required in all forms of investment, but is particularly important in the handling of business funds; a good rate of income is always desirable; convertibility is necessary for a business surplus so that the reserve funds may be converted into cash at any time; and it is of the utmost importance that the security should not shrink materially in quoted price, no matter what changes may take place in financial and business conditions, so that if the need should arise for realizing on the reserve fund, it would be found unimpaired in amount. As explained in a former chapter, this point can not be covered by the selection of securities perfectly safe as to principal and interest, but only by the purchase of short-term obligations.

The point may be illustrated as follows: Let it be supposed that a firm or company has decided to invest $100,000 in the 5-per-cent equipment bonds of a good railroad maturing in three years, which can be obtained at par, merchant's paper then commanding about 5½ per cent. After two years it becomes necessary for the firm to realize on its investment at a time when commercial paper is floated with difficulty on a 6½-per-cent or 7-per-cent basis. Under such money conditions the equipment bonds could be sold on about a 6-per-cent basis, which would mean a price of 99 for a 5-per-cent bond with one year to run. The firm, in liquidating its investment, would therefore lose 1 per cent in principal, but would have received 5 per cent interest for two years, making the net return 4½ per cent. Compare this showing with the result if the bonds when originally bought had had ten years to run instead of three.

After two years, when the firm wished to dispose of its

bonds it might experience some difficulty in doing so in the stringent money market which has been supposed, but even if it succeeded in selling them upon a 6-per-cent basis, that would mean a price of only 93¾ and would represent 6¼-per-cent loss in principal. If it were necessary to sell the bonds upon a higher basis or if the firm had purchased a bond with more than ten years to run, the relative disadvantage of the longer bond would be still more apparent. These points sufficiently demonstrate the importance of buying only short-term securities for the investment of a business surplus. Of course, if money conditions improve instead of becoming worse between the dates of purchase and sale, then a greater profit would be made with the longer-term bond. This, however, should not be allowed to influence the choice, first because it is not the object of a reserve fund to make a speculative profit, and secondly because a firm or corporation is only likely to want to realize upon its reserve fund when money is hard to obtain otherwise, and that is precisely the time when any long-term bond would be apt to show considerable depreciation.

The foregoing considerations indicate a special adaptability on the part of equipment bonds to the usual requirements of a business surplus. The points have been brought out at some length because of the importance of the subject to the average business man. The purpose in concentrating attention upon a single instance has been to illustrate more clearly the principles involved and at the same time to acquaint the business man with details of a highly desirable and somewhat unfamiliar form of security.

IV

REAL-ESTATE MORTGAGES

In the preceding chapter the discussion of railroad bonds was brought to a close. Before passing to the consideration of real-estate mortgages, which is the next form of investment to be taken up, it may be well to review briefly the general principles advanced in the first chapter of this book, in order that the reader may have clearly in mind the main points upon which judgment of the value of investments should be based.

There are five chief points to be considered in the selection of all forms of investment. These are: (1) safety of principal and interest; (2) rate of income; (3) convertibility into cash; (4) prospect of appreciation in intrinsic value; (5) stability of market price.

Keeping these five general factors in mind, the present chapter will discuss real-estate mortgages as a form of investment, both as adapted to the requirements of private funds and of a business surplus.

The average American business man is so familiar with real-estate mortgages that the details may be passed over briefly. A real-estate mortgage, or a bond and mortgage, as it is sometimes called, consists essentially of two parts, a bond or promise to pay a certain sum of money at a future date with interest at a certain rate per annum, and a mortgage or trust deed transferring title and ownership in a piece of real estate, with the provision that the transfer shall be void if the interest is regularly paid and the bond redeemed at maturity. Before advancing money on the security of a mortgage it is necessary to determine whether the title to the property legally vests in the maker of the mortgage; and during the continuance of the mortgage it is necessary to have proof that the taxes and assessments are being regularly paid, and, in the case of improved property, the fire-insurance as well.

The safety of real-estate mortgages, in common with the safety of all obligations, depends upon the margin of security in excess of the amount of the loan. In the case of real-estate mortgages the amount of this margin may be determined without great difficulty. It is only necessary to have the property carefully appraised by an expert in real-estate values. It does not follow, however, because a mortgage has been shown to possess substantial equity, that it is perfectly safe as an investment, unless it satisfies also another condition of great importance. A mortgage may not exceed 50 per cent of the selling value of the real estate pledged, and yet be a poor investment. This point involves a serious objection to real-estate mortgages which sometimes escapes notice.

The holder of a mortgage is at a great disadvantage in regard to the changing value of real estate. If the value of the property upon which he holds a mortgage increases, the additional value enhances the security of the loan, but does not add to the principal which he has invested, while if the value of the property diminishes, not only is the security proportionately lessened, but if the impairment be great, the holder is frequently compelled to take over the property and may suffer loss of principal. In other words, he receives no direct benefit from an increase in the value of the property, but has to stand the larger part of the risk of a decline in its value.

This is not the case with investments represented by negotiable securities subject to changing market quotations. All such securities, railroad bonds for example, are acted on equally by changes in the value of the property which secures them. Except for the influences of money-market conditions, railroad bonds advance with an increase in the value of the property and decline with a decrease in its value. Well-selected bonds usually increase in value with time, and all such increase goes directly to the benefit of the holder. The failure of real-estate mortgages to respond similarly to changes in the value of property places the holder of a mortgage at a great disadvantage.

Owing to this characteristic, real-estate mortgages should be purchased only when general conditions in the real-estate market are distinctly favorable. Not only should the purchaser of a mortgage have sufficient margin of security in the particular piece of property upon which he is loaning money, but he should also be satisfied that general real-estate values are relatively low, that there has been no undue speculation, and that conditions favor an advance rather than a decline in real-estate prices.

No class of property is subject to more rapid changes in value than real estate. After an extensive advance the holder of a mortgage may be insufficiently protected by the equity in the property, even if his mortgage represents only 60 per cent of the current appraised value of the real estate pledged. It may be that the 60 per cent which he has loaned represents the total value or more than the total value a few years before. When a rapid advance in values occurs, tho it may be largely justified by the growth and development of the territory, there is sure to be present an element of speculation which is likely to carry prices beyond the point of reason. When the turn comes and a severe collapse takes place, its effects are extremely disastrous, because, unlike speculation in stocks or commodities, no short selling exists in real estate to temper the fall, and the immobile form of capital makes liquidation impossible. These considerations serve to show the need for great prudence in the purchase of real-estate mortgages. If the investor exercises due care in these particulars, he is reasonably sure of obtaining a very high-grade security; if he neglects these precautions, he may suffer severe loss of principal.

No general figures are available which would indicate the degree of certainty attaching to the payment of interest upon real-estate mortgages. Certain classes of mortgages, such as those secured by unimproved real estate or dwellings, afford no direct security of interest payment other than the threat of foreclosure. Other classes, such as mortgages upon stores, hotels, or office-buildings, are often protected by a large income from the direct operation of the mortgaged premises, thus furnishing a security for the annual interest payment. The margin of protection in these cases varies greatly, so that no general conclusion can be drawn.

The other characteristics of real-estate mortgages may be passed over more briefly. It is generally conceded that mortgages return a higher rate of income than can be obtained upon any other form of investment which affords equal security. This constitutes their chief advantage.

Their chief disadvantage, on the other hand, lies in their entire want of convertibility. There is no market for real-estate mortgages, and except in special instances they can not be readily sold. The fact that they are not subject to quotation prevents them also from holding out any prospect of appreciation in value. Their very deficiency in this respect, however, constitutes an important advantage from another point of view. Since they are not quoted they can not shrink in market price in obedience to changes in financial and business conditions. The buyer of a mortgage is assured that he can carry his mortgage at par through periods when it may be necessary to mark down all negotiable securities subject to changing market quotations. This is frequently a matter of great importance.

The general characteristics of real-estate mortgages may be summarized as follows: (1) When carefully selected and purchased under favorable conditions, great safety of principal and interest; (2) a relatively high return; (3) a low degree of convertibility; (4) no prospect of appreciation in value; and (5) the practical certainty of maintaining the integrity of the principal invested.

Is a security possessing these characteristics a suitable investment for a business surplus? Only to a limited extent. The safety, high return, and assurance against loss in quoted value of principal are all highly desirable qualities for this purpose, but the lack of convertibility is a fatal defect. No consideration is of greater importance in the investment of a business surplus than a high degree of convertibility, so that if the need should arise the investment may be instantly liquidated. The fact that real-estate mortgages can not be readily disposed of makes it practically impossible to employ them for the investment of a business surplus.

Where convertibility is not an essential requirement, and where the want of promise of appreciation in value is not a serious matter, mortgages afford a very desirable form of investment. The characteristics which they possess in an eminent degree—safety, high return, and assurance against loss in quoted value of principal—are exactly suited to the ordinary requirements of savings-banks. Generally speaking, only a small proportion of a savings-bank's assets need be kept in liquid form or readily convertible, and accordingly they find mortgages highly desirable.

For the purpose of private investment the attractiveness of mortgages is not so easy to determine. Ordinarily, fluctuations in quoted values are of no great importance to the private investor, so that the absence of quotation which mortgages enjoy is not especially valuable. Their safety and high return are attractive qualities, but their want of convertibility and of prospect of appreciation in value are drawbacks. On the whole, the private investor may probably employ with advantage a certain part, but not too much of his estate in mortgage investments.

As part of a scientific and comprehensive scheme of investment, the special advantages of real-estate mortgages appear most prominently in the years following a business depression. During such a period real-estate values are usually relatively low, but beginning to advance, so that mortgages present their maximum margin of security. At such a time they compare most favorably with bonds and other investment securities which are subject to changing quotations, because such securities are then apt to be at their highest point under the combined influence of restored confidence and the low money rates which usually prevail. After several years of continued and increasing business prosperity the positions are just reversed.

No discussion of real-estate mortgages would be complete without allusion to the guaranteed mortgages which have been placed upon the market in great quantities within the past few years. Guaranteed mortgages are real-estate mortgages guaranteed as to principal and interest by substantial companies having large capital and surplus. In addition to the guaranty, the companies usually search and guarantee the title, see to it that the taxes, assessments, and insurance are paid, and perform the other services of a real-estate broker. Their compensation varies somewhat, but probably averages ½ per cent—that is, for example, they loan at 5 per cent and sell guaranteed mortgages to the investor at 4½.

The value of the guaranty may be considered from two points of view—first, in the event of a general decline in real-estate values, and, secondly, when a fall occurs in a particular piece of property or in a particular locality.

If a severe decline in real-estate values takes place, affecting all localities, it might become necessary for the holders of guaranteed mortgages to test the value of their guaranties. In such a case the question would arise how far the capital and surplus of the guaranteeing companies would extend in liquidating the mortgages which they had guaranteed. This would depend entirely upon the proportion between the capital and surplus of the companies and the total amount of outstanding mortgages guaranteed. Ordinarily the capital and surplus do not exceed 5 per cent of the mortgages, so that the average guaranty is good for about 5 per cent additional equity. On a piece of property worth $100,000, upon which a guaranteed mortgage of $60,000 exists, the guaranty would be worth $3,000, and would margin the property down to $57,000. This additional equity is of little value. It is probably unlikely that a 40-per-cent depreciation in value will take place, but the guaranty is not needed unless it does, and if it should occur, the depreciation is quite as likely to go to 50 per cent or more as to stop at 43.

From the second point of view the value of the guaranty is much greater. The distribution of risk, as in the case of fire-insurance, protects the holder against loss in the event of a fall in the particular piece of property upon which he holds a mortgage, or even in a particular locality. It can not be said, however, that the records are yet sufficiently complete to form a conclusion as to what is a safe proportion between capital and surplus and outstanding mortgages. Further than that the guaranteeing companies, generally speaking, have been operating since their inception upon a rising market, so that their success hitherto has not been remarkable. Allowing for these drawbacks, however, the private investor, unless so situated as to give personal attention to the details of his investments, will probably do well to purchase his mortgages in guaranteed form.

V

INDUSTRIAL BONDS

Industrial bonds include the obligations of all manufacturing and mercantile companies, and miscellaneous companies of a private character. They form a class quite distinct from railroad bonds or public-utility bonds.

I. Safety of Principal and Interest. The safety of industrial bonds, in common with the safety of all forms of investment, depends upon the margin of security in excess of the amount of the obligation. In the case of industrial bonds the amount of this margin is not always easy to determine. Even when determined, the rule is difficult of application because a margin which may seem insufficient from the point of view of physical valuation may be satisfactory when considered as the equity of a working concern. The indications most to be relied upon in estimating the safety of industrial bonds are as follows:

(a) Value of real estate. The first point to be determined in considering the purchase of an industrial bond is the value of the real estate upon which it is a first mortgage. If the appraised value of the ground, irrespective of the buildings and machinery upon it, is greater by a substantial sum than the amount of the bond issue, the obligation is practically a real-estate mortgage. In such a case, while possibly "slow," i.e., secured by an assets difficult to realize upon—the safety of the bond can hardly be questioned. In judging a bond upon its real-estate value, it is not always safe to take the cost price of the land as shown by the company's books, because frequently the cost upon the books is artificially raised by payment having been made in securities whose market value is less than par, or in other ways. As stated above, judgment should be based upon the appraised value of the land.

If the bond meets this test satisfactorily, the prospective investor may feel reasonably sure that the safety of his principal is not in question, and may buy the bond without anxiety if it satisfies his other requirements. On the other hand, if the bond only partially meets this test, and it appears that some part of its value comes from plant and equipment and from the strength of the company as a working concern, then it is necessary for the investor to consider carefully several other factors.

(b) Net quick assets. The balance-sheet of every industrial company can be divided horizontally into two parts. Its assets are of two kinds—property assets, which are fixt, and current assets, which are fluid. Similarly, its liabilities are of two kinds—capital liabilities and current liabilities. It requires no very extended business experience to pick out the items which make up these totals. Plant and property assets are usually lumped together under the head, "Cost of Property." Current assets include inventories, bills and accounts receivable, agents' balances, marketable securities, and cash on hand and in banks—everything, in short, which can be quickly converted into cash. On the other side of the balance-sheet, capital liabilities are easily determined. They consist of the par amounts of bonds and stocks outstanding. Current liabilities comprise bills and accounts payable, including borrowed money, pay-rolls, and interest and taxes accrued but not due.

The real strength of every industrial concern is to be learned from the figures relating to its current accounts. Property assets and capital liabilities are not of the same significance. If the cost of plant and equipment as shown by the books exceeds its real value, the market usually makes the necessary adjustment by putting a price less than par upon the bonds and stocks.

No such process is possible in the case of the current accounts. If the current liabilities exceed the current assets the company shows a deficit, whatever its surplus may show on the books. On the other hand, if the current assets are greater than the current liabilities, the company possesses a working capital, represented by the difference between the two, and known as net quick assets.

There are three things to consider in connection with net quick assets: First, the proportion between current assets and current liabilities. To put a company in good shape its current assets should be at least twice as great as its current liabilities. Two for one is a fair proportion, tho some companies show as much as six to one. The stronger a company is in this proportion the better.

Secondly, the proportion between net quick assets and bonded debt. The bonded debt should never exceed net quick assets, except when the company possesses real estate, in which case two-thirds of the real-estate value plus the net quick assets should cover the bonds. Some companies do much better than that. One prominent company in this country, altho it possesses real estate of considerable value, has agreed in the indenture securing its bonds to keep net quick assets at all times greater by a substantial margin than the amount of bonds outstanding.

Thirdly, the proportion between net quick assets and the surplus as shown in the balance-sheet. If the capital liabilities exactly balance the property assets, it is plain that the surplus will exactly balance the net quick assets. If the surplus is smaller than net quick assets, it is usually a sign that capital liabilities have been created to provide working capital. Opinions differ as to the wisdom of this course. Generally speaking, it is better to provide working capital by means of a stock issue than to depend upon the banks for accommodation. The exception to this rule occurs in the case of companies that require a great deal of working capital for part of the year and only a little at other times. If they have the best banking connections, such companies may be safe in depending upon their banks to carry them, but if they do so, they should have no bonded or other fixt indebtedness which would prevent their paper from being a first lien upon their entire assets.

If working capital is to be created by the issue of capital liabilities, it is much better that it should be done by stocks than by bonds. The ideal method, however, is to provide only such an amount of working capital at the organization of a company as is necessary for the conduct of its business, and then, as the volume of its business grows, to accumulate the additional amount necessary out of earnings, refraining from the payment of dividends until the fund is complete.

Before leaving the subject of net quick assets, it is well to note the importance of the figure showing the actual amount of current liabilities. If a company has outstanding large amounts of bills and notes payable, it occupies a vulnerable position. Inability to renew maturing notes was the cause of most of the industrial failures of last year.

(c) Net Earnings. The amount of net earnings is of great importance in estimating the strength of an industrial company. The figures for a number of years should be examined to determine whether the earnings are increasing or decreasing, and to discover whether or not the earning power of the company is stable. This will depend largely upon the nature of the article which the company produces or trades in. If its product enjoys a steady demand at a fairly uniform price, it is justifiable that some of its capital should be in the form of bonds; but if its earnings are subject to violent fluctuations due to rapid changes in the price of its product, there is little justification for conducting the business on borrowed money.

In this connection it should always be considered how greatly a falling off in gross earnings will affect net earnings; and the proportion between net earnings and fixt charges should be carefully noted.

In order for an industrial bond to receive favorable consideration, the average yearly net earnings of the company should amount to about three times the annual bond interest, taxes, and sinking funds. The greater the protection is in this respect the better.

(d) Form of Issue. The form in which an industrial bond is issued is a matter of some importance. If the principal of the bond does not become due for a number of years, there is danger that the property will depreciate so far in value as to leave the bond without sufficient margin of protection. There are two ways to overcome this difficulty. One way is to establish a sinking-fund which will retire a certain proportion of the bonds by lot each year. Another way is to issue the bonds in serial form, with a definite instalment maturing every year. In either case the annual sinking-fund or annual instalment should be greater than the probable depreciation so that the margin of security will be constantly increasing.

(e) Management and Control. No question is of greater importance in estimating the strength of an industrial company than the reputation of the men in charge. The ability and integrity of the men who control the policy of the company and the efficiency of the operating officials are the principal factors in the success of an industrial undertaking. Vacillating policies, weakly executed, will ruin the most promising enterprise. This is particularly true in the case of small companies. Every man of business experience will understand the importance of this factor and be guided by it in the selection of industrial securities.

Based upon the foregoing considerations it is of interest to inquire what degree of safety really attaches to the average industrial bond? How far does it meet the foregoing requirements? The question is difficult to answer. Industrial bonds vary greatly in point of safety, some issues possessing great strength and others being highly speculative. No general conclusions can be depended upon, and the investor is forced to consider each issue upon its own merits.

II. Rate of Income. The average net return upon industrial bonds is probably higher than upon any other form of funded corporate obligation. This constitutes one of the chief advantages of industrial bonds.

III. Convertibility. It is impossible to make any general statement in regard to the convertibility of industrial bonds. Some industrial bonds, notably the larger issues of well-known trusts, command a broad and active market. Such bonds can be sold in large amounts at almost any time without seriously affecting the price. On the other hand, small underlying issues of such companies, usually high-grade in point of security, or the obligations of smaller companies, are almost as unmarketable as real-estate mortgages. Between these two extremes all varieties of industrial bonds are to be found. The degree of convertibility which a security possesses is usually a matter of some importance, and the investor should make a careful examination of each bond in this respect.

IV. Prospect of Appreciation in Value. To what extent a bond may improve in security during the time that an investor holds it is of little importance unless the improvement be reflected in the market price of the bond. Only so can the investor take advantage of its appreciation in value. In order for the improvement in security to be reflected in market price and thus add to the principal invested, it is necessary that a bond should possess a fairly active market. For this reason the industrial bonds which hold out the greatest promise of appreciation in value are the larger, more speculative issues, which possess the greatest convertibility. The purchase of such bonds frequently results in substantial profits.

V. Stability of Market Price. The four points above touched upon—safety, rate of income, convertibility, and likelihood of improvement in intrinsic value—are all inherent characteristics of every bond. The likelihood of favorable or unfavorable fluctuation in market price is largely external in its nature and depends upon general financial and business conditions.

As a class, industrial bonds can not be said to possess much stability of market price. Some of the smaller issues enjoy a fictitious stability because of their inactivity, but generally speaking industrial bonds are subject to wide fluctations in accordance with changes in the business outlook.

The foregoing is a summary, necessarily brief and imperfect, of the main points to be considered in judging the value of industrial bonds. The question remains whether such securities are desirable for the investment of a business surplus and of private funds.

Except in special cases industrial bonds are not suitable for a business surplus. It is impossible to find an industrial bond which combines all the characteristics necessary for that purpose. The requirements are great safety of principal and interest, a relatively high return, ready convertibility, and stability of market price. Many industrial bonds can be found which combine two of these requirements, some even which combine three, but the full combination, if it exists at all, is unknown to the writer.

In addition, the principle of distribution of risk should prevent one industrial company from investing its reserve funds in the securities of another industrial company.

For private investment the case is somewhat different. A man of good business judgment, who desires to obtain a high yield for which he is prepared to sacrifice something in the way of convertibility and prospect of appreciation in value, may buy the underlying issues of strong companies with every confidence in the safety of his principal. Again, the investor who wants a high yield and quick convertibility, who is prepared to take a business man's risk and to sacrifice stability of market price, may make a large profit by buying second-grade industrial bonds. No investor, however, should deceive himself with the idea that any industrial bond will satisfy all the requirements of the ideal investment.

VI
PUBLIC-UTILITY BONDS

It was a common saying among bond-dealers a few years ago that the day of the municipal bond had passed, the day of the railroad bond was passing, and the day of the public-utility bond was to be. Municipal bonds were selling at fancy prices in consequence of the low rates for money which then prevailed, and railroad bonds appeared to be following in their wake. Public-utility bonds alone afforded a satisfactory yield, and it was felt that the investing public would be forced to turn to them.

This prediction, like many others which were based upon the assumption of continued ease in money, was destined to be unfulfilled. Almost immediately there appeared an added demand for capital, and in the face of this demand, supplies of capital which had before seemed ample became suddenly scarce. Money rates rose rapidly and as a necessary consequence municipal and railroad bonds fell in price to a point where their net return was commensurate with that obtained from the loaning of free capital. The investment situation was thus completely reversed. It was no longer a question as to what form of security investors must seek in order to obtain a satisfactory yield, but rather could the highest grade of municipal and railroad bonds be floated at any price. Under these circumstances the contemplated necessity of turning to public-utility bonds never arose, and the general investing public remains for the most part unfamiliar with their elements of strength and of weakness.

The term "public-utility company" denotes a private corporation supplying public needs under authority of a public franchise. The franchise may be of definite date or perpetual, and may be partial or exclusive.

Public-utility companies include street-railway, gas, electric-light and power, and water companies. Properly speaking, telephone companies should also be included, but they are not usually regarded as belonging to the class of public-service corporations.

It is impossible, within the limits of a single chapter, to discuss each kind of company separately. The investment value of street-railway bonds will be here considered, and it is felt that the general principles advanced, with slight modifications of detail, will be found equally applicable to a judgment of other forms of public-service securities.

I. Safety of Principal and Interest. In order to determine the safety of a street-railway company's bonds, the company must be subjected to a threefold examination, physical, financial, and political.

An examination must be made into the extent and condition of the physical property in order to ascertain whether the bonded debt is secured by property having a real market value in excess of the face amount of bonds issued. The first point to be determined is the extent and valuation of the company's real estate. If the appraised value of the land upon which power-houses and car-barns have been erected is alone greater than the amount of bonds outstanding, the investigation need go no further, for the bonds, in such a case, would be practically a real-estate mortgage. In most instances, however, this is very far from being the case; and after careful appraisal of the real estate it is then necessary to make a careful valuation of the other physical property; namely, power-plants, depots, car-sheds, roadway, and equipment.

It is usually impossible for the average investor to make such an examination himself, nor is it likely that he would possess sufficient technical knowledge to render his investigation of much value. For an accurate estimate of the value of a street-railway's physical property, it is usually necessary to depend upon the expert opinion of a trained engineer. It is a matter of regret that the average street-railway report can not be relied upon to furnish an accurate valuation of the physical property; and it is accordingly customary for careful bond-dealers, when they contemplate taking an issue of street-railway bonds for distribution among their clients, to have the property examined by a competent engineer, whose report then determines for them the question of taking the issue.

Disregarding the figures which show the cost of property and equipment upon the company's books, the engineer proceeds to make a careful estimate of the replacement value of the property, including real estate. If the result of the examination shows that the property could not be duplicated for the amount of the bond issue, the company occupies an unusually strong position—altho even in such a case some part of the value of the bonds comes from the strength of the company as a going concern.

In most cases, however, it is probably found that the bond issue is in excess of the value of real estate and the replacement value of the physical property, the balance representing a capitalization of the franchise.

To determine the real value of the franchise or franchises is a difficult matter and involves the whole question of the company's relations with the community which it serves and with the local lawmaking bodies.

The first question which arises is whether the franchise is perpetual or for a definite time, and the second whether it is partial or exclusive. Franchises vary greatly in these respects. Sometimes a franchise, apparently partial, is practically exclusive, owing to the fact that all the available space in the streets is already occupied by the company's own tracks. If the franchises of a company are limited as to time, it is expedient, if not imperative, that the bonds should mature before the expiration of the franchises.

If the company whose bonds are under examination satisfactorily passes this physical test—if it possesses real estate of considerable value, if the replacement value of the property is as great or nearly as great as the amount of the bonds, and if the franchises, while perhaps not perpetual or exclusive, are yet of longer duration than the bonds and render successful competition unlikely—the next step may then be taken; that is to say, an examination of the company's financial condition and earning capacity may be made.

The amount of its gross earnings should be examined and the figures scrutinized for a number of years back to discover whether its earnings are increasing or decreasing. The position in which the company stands for obtaining new traffic must be noted, and some estimate must be made of the stability of its earning power. In this connection the relations of the company to the public are of great importance. It must be learned whether the company follows the policy of conciliating or ignoring public sentiment.

The net earnings of the company must then be examined. This involves a criticism of operating expenses. The payments of the road must be analyzed to determine whether the proper amounts have been expended for renewal of track, replenishment of rolling stock, and other improvement sufficient to keep the property in good physical condition. This is the most intricate subject in the investigation of a street-railway property. Unless proper allowance be made for depreciation, in addition to the expenses of direct operation, it is only a question of time before the strongest company will become bankrupt.

Deterioration of plant and equipment, which goes on constantly, can only be offset in two ways: one is out of earnings and the other is out of the security-holders—that is, by decreases in the market value of the securities. The first takes prosperity or courage; the second leads to bankruptcy. It is difficult to measure depreciation accurately, but a safe rule is to write off ten per cent of gross earnings each month for depreciation. In this way the charge for depreciation will be proportionate to the traffic, which provides automatic adjustment.

If the net earnings, after making this allowance for depreciation, and after providing all expenses of operation including ordinary repairs, amount to as much as twice the interest charges upon the bonds outstanding, it is probable that the bonds may be taken with safety.

Before finally determining the question, however, certain political factors must be taken into consideration. The relations of the company to the leaders of the dominant political party must be investigated. The likelihood of agitation looking toward a reduction of fares must be considered and the possibility of increase in taxes (if below the legal limit) must be weighed. The probable attitude of the legislature on the question of renewing the franchises when they expire must be considered. In general, it must be learned whether any real ground of contention exists between the company on the one hand and the public and its representatives on the other, because it is inevitable that the company will weaken its independence of position by too close a connection with politics, and that the physical property will suffer if there is any lack of uninterrupted attention to it.

Finally one other thing should be investigated—the amount of the accident account and its proportion to the net earnings of the company. On small lines a single case of heavy damages will sometimes make serious inroads upon the earnings.

The foregoing is a summary, necessarily brief and

imperfect, but true in its essential outlines, of the main points which should be considered in judging the safety of street-railway bonds. The question remains, how far does the average street-railway company satisfy these requirements? Broadly speaking, street-railway bonds are not yet to be classed in the first rank of investment securities. The troubles which have come to a head in the financial operations of the traction systems in New York and Chicago are typical of troubles which are likely to occur elsewhere from the same general causes— overcapitalization in the first place and insufficient allowance for depreciation in the second place. In both New York and Chicago the crisis was hastened by open and obvious overcapitalization, which is almost inevitable when many independent lines are merged into one system. The same trouble, however, is apt to occur in other traction systems where this evil appeared less flagrant at the outset.

The advantages of electricity over horsepower naturally led to the multiplication of electric street lines, as the system ten or fifteen years ago passed beyond the experimental stage. As in all new enterprises, speculation ran ahead of the reality and financing built upon oversanguine calculations has too often had difficulty in squaring accounts when brought face to face with facts. In most of the calculations insufficient allowance was made for the wear and tear of service; in other words, for renewal of road and equipment. After a few years' test of earnings against expenses, it became evident that a proper allowance for depreciation of plant would show a heavy deficit in the income account. In most cases therefore no allowance or only a meager one was made. For a time this method of bookkeeping proved less disastrous than might have been expected owing to the rapid growth of population and business in American cities. It was possible in many cases to consider the enhanced value given to the franchise by growth of business as an offset to the depreciation of tracks and equipment. In so far also as the plant was kept up to a high degree of efficiency by charging the expense of repairs to operating expenses, the absence of a depreciation account was partially offset.

With the progress of recent years, however, a new factor has been entering into the problem which promises to make the situation still more serious for the traction systems. This new factor is the rise in prices and wages. Temporarily the influence of this factor may be checked by diminished business activity, but when normal conditions are restored, it will commence to act again upon the railways with accumulated effect.

In most cases a proposition to increase the standard street-railway fare above five cents as an offset to the increased operating expenses would be so revolutionary a proposal that it could hardly be carried through. With the line of cost converging upon the line of receipts and with no proper allowance made for depreciation, the traction systems of the country seem to be facing a difficult problem. In the long run it can not be doubted that the problem will be met and solved in a way to afford justice alike to the public who use the cars and to the capitalists who have made street traction on a large scale possible, but in the meantime the investor who desires perfect safety should exercise great care and discrimination in his purchases of street-railway obligations.

II. Rate of Income. As a general rule, street-railway bonds in common with the obligations of all public-service corporations sell upon about the same income basis as high-grade industrial bonds—that is to say, under normal conditions they return considerably more than railroad or municipal bonds.

III. Convertibility. It is difficult to speak of the convertibility of public-utility bonds as a class for the reason that they differ widely from one another in this respect. In general, it is certainly more difficult to dispose of public-utility bonds than railroad bonds. They do not possess sufficient convertibility to justify their purchase by any one who may need to realize quickly on his holdings.

IV. Prospect of Appreciation in Value. Public-utility bonds, except such issues as are convertible into stock, possess little prospect of appreciation in value. It was pointed out above that depreciation is not properly allowed for, and it is very difficult for the securities to advance in the face of this obstacle.

V. Stability of Market Price. The bonds of public-service corporations are relatively more stable than railroad bonds because their earnings are not subject to the fluctuations which occur in railroad properties between years of prosperity and years of depression. At the same time, it should be pointed out that their stability of price is largely fictitious, owing to the comparative inactivity of the issues. In other words, while the quotation may be maintained, it is usually difficult to sell any large quantity of a public-service corporation's bonds in a period of financial disturbance, while railroad bonds are more easily liquidated even if at a sacrifice.

The question remains, do public-utility bonds afford a desirable security for the investment of a business surplus and of private funds? In regard to the former, it may be said at once that public-utility bonds do not meet the necessary conditions. The security is too doubtful, the convertibility is too small, and the stability of price too uncertain.

For private investment the case is somewhat different. Keeping in mind the desirability of diversifying investments and admitting the attractiveness of investing in a class of property whose earnings are comparatively stable, it seems clear that public-utility bonds can not be dismissed without consideration. When a company is found whose property is substantially equal in real value to its bonded debt, whose allowance for depreciation is ample, whose franchises are satisfactory, whose earning capacity is large, and whose management is capable and upright, the investor is justified in giving careful consideration to its issues. Unless all these points are found to be satisfactory, however, the investor should content himself with some other form of security. For some years to come it is to be feared that many of our public-service corporations will suffer from the war of discordant elements—disregard of the rights of the public on the part of the management and socialistic agitation for control on the part of the community. Until these warring factions are reconciled and the questions at issue adjusted with fairness to the security-holders and the public, the investor should be most prudent in his purchases of public-utility obligations.

VII
MUNICIPAL BONDS

The previous chapters have considered, in turn, the investment value of railroad bonds, real-estate mortgages, industrial bonds, and public-utility bonds. The desirability of each of these different classes of security has been judged in accordance with the general principles laid down in the introductory chapter; that is to say, each class has been analyzed in relation to safety, rate of income, convertibility, prospect of appreciation in value and stability of market price. The same determining factors must now be applied to a judgment of government, State, and municipal bonds.

Bonds issued by a national government, by a State, or by a municipality are based primarily on some form of the power of taxation, tho the bonds are usually tax exempt within the political unit which creates them.

When the power of taxation is unlimited, as in the case of the national government and the sovereign States, there can be no question as to the ability of the political unit to meet its obligation, and the question becomes entirely one of good faith. It is probable that the obligations of the

United States Government, by reason of the fact that the per-capita debt of the country is so small, the wealth of the country so great, and the good faith of the American people so clearly established, represent the highest type of security to be found in the world. It is quite possible, therefore, that the 2-per-cent United States Consols would sell in any case at a relatively higher price than the obligations of any other country, but it can not be denied that the chief reason which causes them to sell at the remarkably high price which they have attained is the fact that they are required by national banks as security for circulation. This fact is doubtless the controlling element in their market position, and at once accounts for their special strength and removes them from the field of private investment.

Only less secure than United States bonds are the obligations of the sovereign States of the Union. State bonds usually sell upon a basis which may be taken as the equivalent of pure interest, with no element of risk or speculation involved. The obligations of different States sell at different prices, in accordance with market conditions and the relations of supply and demand, but there can be no question of the equal ability of all States to pay their obligations. Repudiation of State debts has occurred in our history, but only in cases where an overwhelming majority of the citizens were opposed to the creation of the debt at the time of its issue, but lacked the means to control the situation. Such instances are chiefly to be found in the case of the so-called carpet-bag governments of the Southern States after the Civil War.

Municipal bonds—i.e., the bonds of cities, counties, and townships—are indirectly a first lien upon all taxable property in the municipality, and take precedence of every form of mortgage or judgment lien. This lien is enforced through a tax levy to meet interest and principal, and this tax levy the courts will compel in the rare cases in which a municipality attempts to repudiate a valid bond. This priority of the tax lien is the foundation of the prime position of municipal bonds. The case rarely occurs where a bond held valid by the courts proves uncollectable if sufficient taxing power existed when the bond was issued to provide for its redemption. It is only when the municipality itself diminishes in population and taxable property to the vanishing-point that such a default can occur. An investor can judge for himself as to the likelihood of such a catastrophe in any particular community, and can feel sure that his bond, if valid and protected by a sufficient taxing power, is as secure in its principal and interest as the municipality which issues it is secure in its continued existence. The following are the chief points which should be considered in the investigation of a municipal bond: (1) The proportion which the total debt of the municipality bears to the assessed valuation of the property subject to taxation. Usually a maximum rate is fixt by constitutional provision which rarely exceeds 10 per cent. (2) The purpose of issue. This must be a proper and suitable one. (3) The proceedings under which the bonds were issued. These proceedings, the form of bonds, their execution, and their legal details must be in full compliance with the law.

If these points are found to be satisfactory, the investor may rest content that no other form of security is so greatly safeguarded and that his bond ranks upon a substantial equality with government and State obligations.

The rate of income to be derived from investment in municipal bonds varies in accordance with the obligations selected. Like other forms of security, municipal bonds are controlled by market conditions, and their price is determined by the relations of supply and demand, and by adjustment to prevailing money rates. While differing only moderately from one another in point of safety and income return, municipal bonds may be divided into two distinct classes in accordance with the degree of convertibility which they possess. Some municipal bonds possess great convertibility; others almost none. The feature which chiefly determines the activity or inactivity of a municipal issue is the size and importance of the municipality, together with the amount of bonds which it has outstanding. The bonds of large and important cities, whose outstanding debt reaches considerable proportions, usually possess great activity. They are constantly traded in and command a broad market because dealers are willing to buy or sell them in blocks at prices within a fraction of 1 per cent apart.

On the other hand, the bonds of counties, townships, and small cities are usually quite inactive. Transactions rarely occur in them, dealers do not make a market in them, and they can be sold only to genuine investors. It is often impossible to have them even quoted.

At first sight, it would appear that active municipal bonds would be much more desirable, but inactive municipals possess a special advantage which the active ones do not enjoy. They possess more stability of market price. It is true that their stability of value is due to the fact that they are not traded in or quoted and is, therefore, largely fictitious, but nevertheless it accomplished a useful purpose. It enables the investor to carry inactive municipals at cost price upon his books through periods in which active market bonds would require to be marked down in conformity with prevailing market prices. No other class of investment except real-estate mortgages possesses to the same degree this quality of price stability. For many classes of buyers—savings-banks, for example— stability of price is a consideration of prime importance. The preservation of the savings-bank's surplus and, indeed, the continued solvency of the institution depend upon maintaining the integrity of the principal which it has invested. A savings-bank requires, also, great safety of principal and interest; i.e., the certainty that principal and interest instalments will be paid at maturity. It needs only a fair but not high yield, and it does not need to place emphasis upon convertibility or prospect of appreciation in value. Comparison of these requirements with the characteristics of inactive municipal bonds discloses a striking adaptability on their part to the real needs of the case. As a consequence, it is not surprizing to discover that inactive municipals are greatly sought by savings-banks.

The desirability of inactive municipals for savings-bank investment was never more forcibly illustrated than on the first of last January, when the savings-banks came to make up their annual statements. Broadly speaking, there can be no doubt that they were saved by the large quantity of inactive municipals and real-estate mortgages which they carried. Had any considerable portion of their assets consisted of railroad bonds and active municipals, upon which they should have had to write off a loss of ten to fifteen points, their solvency would almost certainly have been impaired.

But we are chiefly concerned in these pages with the advantages and disadvantages of different forms of investment from the point of view of a business man, both for the investment of his business surplus and of his private funds. Do municipal bonds, either active or inactive, conform to the requirements of the business surplus? It can not be said that they do. Municipal bonds possess either convertibility without stability of price or stability of price without convertibility. Both qualities are necessary for a business surplus. The only form of municipal security which is at all adapted for the investment of a business surplus is a short-term issue of an active municipal bond. If it has only a very few years to run, its constant approach to maturity will invest it with the necessary stability of price. But even in this case equal safety and equal stability of price combined with a higher yield can probably be found in some high-grade railroad issue—either a short-term mortgage or equipment bond.

For private investment the case is somewhat different. Enough has been said in the preceding chapters to impress upon the reader the importance of buying securities only in accordance with his real requirements. If any investor, after careful comparison of the characteristics of municipal bonds, either active or inactive, with his necessities, decides that he can more closely satisfy his requirements with municipals than with any other form of security, he should not hesitate to purchase them. It is the opinion of the writer, however, that a thorough survey of the field of investment will generally disclose to the investor some security in either the railroad or corporation field which will suit his requirements as well as the municipal bond and at the same time provide him with a greater income.

VIII
STOCKS

Passing to the consideration of stocks as investments, it is necessary at the outset that the reader should have clearly in mind the fundamental difference between stocks and bonds. This distinction was drawn in the introductory chapter, but it will be well to amplify it here, even at the risk of carrying the reader over familiar ground.

The distinction between bonds and stocks is that between promises to pay and equities. Bonds, loans on collateral, and real-estate mortgages represent some one's promise to pay a sum of money at a future date; and if the promise be valid and the security ample, the holder of the promise will be paid the money on the date due. Stocks, on the other hand, represent only a beneficial interest or residuary share in the assets and profits of a working concern after payment of its obligations and fixt charges. The value of the residuary share may be large or small, may increase or diminish, but in no case can the holder of such a share require any one, least of all the company itself, to take his share off his hands at the price he paid for it, or, indeed, at any price. If a man buys a $1,000 railroad bond, he knows that the railroad, if solvent, will pay him $1,000 in cash when the bond matures, but if he buys a share of railroad stock his only chance of getting his money back, if he should wish it, is that some one else will want to buy his share from him at the price he paid for it or more. If he buys a bond he becomes a creditor of the company, without voice in its management, but entitled to receive his principal and interest when due under pain of forfeiture of the security which the company made over to the trustee to insure payment. If he buys stock, he becomes a partner in a business enterprise, exercising his proportionate share in the direction of the company's affairs, and sharing ratably in its profits and losses. In the one case he buys a promise to pay and in the other an equity.

This distinction, which appears plainly marked in theory, has been much obscured in recent years by the influence of two factors. As the country grew in size, the large corporations—the railroads, for example—required greater capital in order to provide facilities for the handling of their growing business. It was impossible to provide this capital wholly by means of bond issues without destroying the proportion between bonds and stocks, which alone could give to the bondholders the protection of a substantial equity. It was therefore necessary to obtain a large part of the capital required in the form of stock. The railway-managers were thus confronted with a difficult problem. It was imperative that they should obtain more capital, and it was impossible to dispose of sufficient stock on the basis of a speculative risk in a business venture. It was therefore necessary for the railway-managers to emphasize, as far as possible, the investment character of their stock, and various expedients were adopted to accomplish this purpose. In some cases preferred stocks were created or resulted from reorganizations, which possess a first lien upon the assets after payment of the obligations, and which were entitled to a certain stipulated dividend before the common stock obtained any distribution from the earnings. In this way the railway-managers created a compromise security which could be regarded as a stock, and would thus provide equity from the bondholders' point of view, and, at the same time, one which could be disposed of to investors. In other cases, which were probably more numerous, railway-managers attempted to give their stock an investment value through stability of income return. In good years when the company earned 10 or 15 per cent on its stock, their policy was to pay only 5 or 6 per cent in dividends, and hold the rest in their surplus fund in order to have the means of paying the same dividends the next year if only 2 or 3 per cent should be earned. By giving their stock stability of income return they hoped and expected to give it some stability of market price, and thus make it attractive to genuine investors. The effect of this policy was unquestionably successful, and one after another the stocks of our more important transportation systems and other large undertakings passed into the hands of investors.

The successful adoption of this policy on the part of the railway-managers and other captains of industry has had one curious effect which was not contemplated by the originators of the movement, and which brings us to the second influence mentioned above as having tended to obscure the distinction between bonds and stocks. When a case has been brought before the courts in which the contention was advanced that the charges of the railway or public-service corporation were too high, the courts appear to have taken the ground that stocks and bonds should be classed together in order to determine the aggregate capitalization of the company, and that the justice or injustice of the contention that the charges are too high should be determined by ascertaining whether if the charges were made lower the net earnings would still be sufficient to pay a fair return on the total capital invested. This is the general line of reasoning pursued by the courts, both in the case of the Consolidated Gas

Company in New York and the Pennsylvania Railroad in Pennsylvania. The effect of this attitude on the part of the courts has been to obscure still more greatly the real distinction between bonds and stocks. It is too early as yet to judge what will be the final outcome of the changed attitude toward stocks, but it can not be doubted that the present tendency of opinion on the subject, so far as large corporations are concerned, is to limit the return on stocks to a strictly investment basis, instead of leaving the stockholders free to reap all possible profit from their business venture subject to the restraints of competition.

The adoption of this attitude by the courts should be a matter for serious consideration on the part of present and prospective stockholders. If the maximum return on stock is to be limited to 6 per cent, or any fair investment basis, and charges reduced to consumers so that they obtain the benefit of any greater earning power, it would appear that the stockholders occupy an undesirable position. With their possible profits limited, but with no fixt return insured to them and no guaranty against possible loss, it can not be held that the purchase of stock seems attractive.

These questions, however, will doubtless be settled in the long run in justice both to the public and to the stockholders, and in the meantime the stocks of our large and successful railway and industrial corporations, which have attained a certain stability and permanence of value, are entitled to consideration when investments are contemplated. It is not worth while to lay down rules for judging the investment value of such stocks, because the general principles advanced in the preceding chapters will be found sufficient for a judgment of their values.

One class of stocks, however, deserves special mention. Bank and trust-company stocks possess one characteristic in higher degree than other classes of stock. Owing to the general practise of self-regulated banking institutions to distribute only about one-half their earnings in dividends and to credit the rest to surplus account, a steady rise is assured in the book value of the stock. No other class of stock possesses quite the same promise of appreciation in value. Bank and trust-company stocks are especially sought by wealthy men, who can forego something in the way of income return for the sake of increasing the amount of their principal. The general characteristics of bank stocks are great safety, a low rate of income, limited convertibility, and practical certainty of appreciation in value.

With the present chapter the discussion of specific forms of investments has come to an end. The next and concluding chapter will explain the general principles which control the market movements of all negotiable securities, and will endeavor to point out the indications which may be relied upon in determining whether or not given conditions are favorable for the purchase of securities.

IX
MARKET MOVEMENTS OF SECURITIES

There is no question connected with the investment of money more important than the ability to judge whether general market conditions are favorable for the purchase of securities.

After learning how to judge the value of every form of investment, a man may still be unsuccessful in the investment of money unless he acquires also a firm grasp upon the general principles which control the price movements of securities. By this it is not meant that a man needs to have an intimate knowledge of technical market conditions whereby to estimate temporary fluctuations of minor importance, but rather that he should have clearly in mind the causes which operate to produce the larger swings of prices. If an investor acquires such a knowledge, he is enabled to take advantage of large price movements in such a way as materially to increase his income, and, at the same time, avoid carrying upon his books securities which may have cost much more than their current market quotations. If he can recognize the indications which point to the beginning of a pronounced upward swing in securities, and if he can equally recognize the signs which indicate that the movement has culminated, he can liquidate the securities which he bought at the inception of the rise or transfer them to some short-term issues whose near approach to maturity will render them stable in price, allowing the downward swing to proceed without disturbing him. It is not expected, of course, that the average business man will be able to realize completely this ideal of investment, but it is hoped that the following analysis will give him a clearer conception of the principles involved.

Broadly speaking, the market movements of all negotiable securities are controlled by two influences, sometimes acting in opposition to each other and sometimes in concert. One of these influences is the loaning rate of free capital; the other is the general condition of business. A low rate of interest or the likelihood of low rates has the effect of stimulating security prices, because banks and other money-lending institutions are forced into the investment market when they can not loan money to advantage. Conversely, a high rate of interest or the prospect of high rates has the effect of depressing prices, because banking institutions sell their securities in order to lend the money so released. The automatic working of this process tends to produce a constant adjustment between the yields upon free and invested capital. When money rates are low, securities tend to advance to the point where the return upon them is no greater than that derived from the loaning of free capital. When rates are high, securities tend to decline to a point where the return is as great. This explains the influence of the first factor.

The other factor is the general condition of business. Good business conditions, or the promise of good conditions, tend to advance security prices, because they indicate larger earnings and a stronger financial condition. Poor business conditions, or an unpromising outlook, have the reverse effect.

The larger movements of security prices are always the resultant of the interaction of these two forces. When they work together the effect is irresistible, as when low interest rates and the prospect of good business conditions occur together, or when high money rates occur in the face of an indicated falling off in business activity. At such times all classes of securities swing together. For the most part, however, money rates and business conditions are opposed in their influence, rates being low when business is bad and high when business is good. Usually the worse business conditions become, the easier money grows; while the more active business becomes, the higher money rates rise. The effect of this antagonism between the controlling causes is to produce movements of different proportions and sometimes in different directions in different classes of securities. High-grade bonds may be declining, middle-grade bonds remaining stationary, and poor bonds advancing, all at the same time. This serves to give a very irregular appearance to the security markets, and appears to justify the widely held opinion that security prices are a pure matter of guesswork, and that they are controlled only by manipulation and special influences. A clear conception of the nature of the influences which are always silently at work reconciles these apparent inconsistencies and makes it plain that general price movements are determined by laws as certain in their operation as the laws of nature.

This may be illustrated by a single example. Let us assume that interest rates are low and business conditions bad with prospect of still lower interest rates and still more unpromising business conditions. What will be the effect upon different classes of securities? High-grade bonds, such as choice municipals, whose safety can not be impaired by any extent of depression in business, will advance because their market price is influenced almost wholly by money rates. If their interest is certain to be paid, no matter what business conditions may become, they can not be greatly affected by a reduction of earnings, and consequently the influence of low money rates is left to act practically alone. Middle-grade bonds, such as second-class railroad issues, will remain almost stationary, low money rates tending to advance their price and the fear of decreased earnings tending to depress them. The lowest grade of bonds and stocks, whose margin of security even in good times is not very great, will probably suffer in price because the fear of default in interest and of reduction in dividends will operate much more strongly than the mere stimulus of low interest rates. Of course, securities can not be clearly separated into these three classes, but shade imperceptibly into one another. The classification is adopted only for purposes of illustration.

Up to this point we have been concerned merely in showing that the market movements of negotiable securities are controlled by the influence of certain factors. A more important question now remains to be considered, viz.: whether the effect of these two influences is to produce general swings in prices which may be depended upon with comparative certainty, and, if so, what indications are afforded to the investor of the commencement or culmination of such a movement. The answer must be that the combined effect of the two influences described is to produce definite and regular swings in prices, and that the indications which define the movements are not difficult to follow.

A general survey of the history of every industrial nation reveals the fact that business conditions undergo alternate periods of prosperity and depression extending in clearly defined cycles of substantially uniform length. By tracing the usual course of interest rates and of business conditions throughout one of these cycles, a general idea can be formed of the way in which the joint influences operate to produce price movements. To what extent the course of interest rates is a cause as well as a result of changing business conditions, we shall not attempt here to estimate, but will be content to note carefully the general course which rates for money pursue throughout the cycles. Immediately after a financial crisis, which usually closes an era of great business prosperity, money rates become abnormally easy. Within a few months from the climax of the crisis, money accumulates in enormous volume in financial centers. This is caused by the great diminution of business activity which renders unnecessary a large part of the circulating medium that was formerly required to transact the greater volume of business. To the extent to which this accumulation of money merely reflects a redundancy of currency as distinguished from real liquid capital, it can have little effect in encouraging the resumption of business activity. As time passes, however, and economies in operation commence to make themselves manifest, and especially as waste and extravagance are curtailed, the country as a whole commences to accumulate real liquid capital; that is to say, its total production leaves a surplus over the amount of consumption. In the state of business feeling which has been pictured, the undertaking of new business ventures or additions to existing properties would not be approved, so that the surplus wealth created finds its way into bank deposits as liquid capital. The competitive attempt to loan this capital at a time when borrowers are few produces merely nominal interest rates. This continues for some time. It is only gradually as confidence returns and as the spirit of initiative begins to reassert itself that some part of the liquid capital created each year is diverted into fixt forms. Here and there some enterprising group of men will develop a mine, lay a new piece of railway, or make some addition to an existing undertaking. For some length of time, however, the liquid capital of the country not only remains unimpaired, but is continually increasing. After a time a change comes. The annual surplus of production, tho larger than before, is only sufficient to provide for the new undertakings which the growing optimism demands. Interest rates rise moderately in response to the added demand for capital. A few years further along, as business activity increases and success appears plainly to wait upon new ventures, the demand for new capital with which to develop increased facilities and new enterprises exceeds the annual supply of wealth created. Prosperity having increased, another factor commences to assert itself. The spirit of economy and thrift which had prevailed throughout the years of depression gives place to extravagance, the demand for luxuries, and other unproductive forms of expenditure. While the total production is much greater than in the lean years, the margin of production is not proportionately as great, and this amount is insufficient to meet the demands upon it. The supplies of liquid capital stored up during the years of depression are resorted to, and they serve to provide the new capital for a few additional years. Interest rates at once reflect the encroachment upon stored-up capital, and their rise gives the first real warning of the country's true position. The optimistic business men do not heed the warning. After exhausting all the real capital available in the country, they proceed to borrow extensively from foreigners or from government banks—in this country from the national government through bank deposits. Every step which can be taken to induce foreigners to part with their capital is resorted to. If foreigners will not buy long-term bonds, short-term notes are created. If the foreigners refuse these, they are asked to make loans secured by the new bonds and notes. The rates of interest offered are so attractive that considerable sums are usually obtained, and the pressure of business activity continues further. Finally the day of reckoning arrives when some incident, usually unimportant in itself, first suggests to the lenders of money that their debtors whom they know to be overextended may not be able to pay their loans. The attempt to collect their loans produces a financial crisis which brings to an end the period of prosperity.

The foregoing is a description of the more important stages through which business conditions pass from crisis to crisis. Different cycles vary in particular details, but all agree in essential outlines. Sometimes special influences are at work which operate to shorten or prolong the cycle. The approach of a crisis will be retarded by inflation of the currency, for the excess finds its way into bank vaults and increases the volume of loanable credit. The effect of such inflation, however, is wholly disastrous, because the addition to the supply of capital is fictitious, not real, and only defers the day of reckoning for a greater catastrophe. On the other hand, the approach of a crisis can be greatly hastened by wars, conflagrations, and other agencies which destroy capital, and by attacks upon capital and the conduct of corporate business, for such attacks tend to render capital timid and produce the same effect as a violent curtailment of the supply. These are only some of the many influences which might become operative, but they serve to show the necessity for careful consideration of all the factors at work if a true conception of the condition and tendencies of business is to be formed.

From the general account given above of the successive phases of a credit cycle, it is possible to summarize the course of interest rates and the course of business conditions. Money rates become suddenly easy after a crisis, remain low or grow easier for a period of several years, and then rise continuously until the next crisis, advancing with great rapidity toward the close of the cycle. Business conditions remain poor or grow worse a few years after a crisis. Liquidation is taking place, prices are going down, and the uncertainty of the outlook causes diminished activity. Thereafter, however, conditions improve and activity increases with fair uniformity until it reaches the high tension of the period immediately preceding the crisis. The course of interest rates and the course of business conditions may both be deflected by the operation of special influences, but the general tendencies are substantially as outlined. The result of the operation of these joint factors may be traced in the market movements of any class of security desired. For the sake of simplicity, let us consider their effect in producing the market swings of the highest grade of investment issues and of the lowest grade, those which are affected only by money rates and those which are affected almost wholly by business conditions.

Emerging from the strain of the crisis at their lowest point, high-grade bonds, such as the best municipal and railroad issues, advance rapidly as interest rates decline, continuing their advancing tendency throughout the period of business depression which follows upon the heels of the crisis. As business conditions improve, their position, while perfectly secure before, is further strengthened and an added stimulus is given to their rise. About the middle of the cycle when the business outlook is very promising, and before interest rates have sustained any material advance, the prices of high-grade bonds are usually at their highest point. From that time forward they commence to decline, in spite of the increasing prosperity of the country, under the influence of rising money rates. They make their lowest prices in the midst of the crisis, when the strain upon capital is greatest and the outlook for business most unpromising.

The lowest grade of bonds, on the other hand (whose margin of security is least), do not commence to recover materially in price, in spite of the influence of low money rates during the hard times which follow the crisis, the influence of reduced earnings and the fear of default of interest holding them in check. As the outlook becomes brighter, they advance rapidly and continue to improve in price so long as they yield more than current money rates.

At some point, difficult to determine in advance but usually well along toward the end of the cycle, they reach their high point and thereafter decline under the influence of the growing stringency in money.

Between these two extremes, every class of security is to be found. The better ones will tend to resemble, in their market movements, the course pursued by the choicest bonds; the poorer ones will approximate the lowest class. In every case, however, unless special influences operate to produce variations, the market swing of a given security should be easily conjectured by an investor who gives careful attention to the relative weight which is likely to attach to each determining influence.

CREATING CAPITAL
MONEY-MAKING AS AN AIM IN BUSINESS

By
FREDERICK L. LIPMAN

This series will contain essays by representative scholars and men of affairs dealing with the various phases of the moral law in its bearing on business life under the new economic order, first delivered at the University of California on the Weinstock foundation.

CREATING CAPITAL
MONEY-MAKING AS AN AIM IN BUSINESS

The object of this paper is to discuss money-making; to examine its prevalence as an aim among people generally and the moral standards which obtain among those who consciously seek to make money.

The desire to make money is common to most men. Stronger or weaker, in some degree it is present in the mind of nearly every one. Now, how far does this desire grow to be an aim or object in our lives, and to what extent is such an aim a worthy one?

The typical money-maker as commonly pictured in our imagination is a narrow, grasping, selfish individual who has chosen to follow lower rather than higher ideals and who often is tempted, and always may be tempted, to employ illegitimate means for the attainment of his ends. The aims he has adopted are made to stand in opposition to the practice of certain virtues. Thus we contrast profits and patriotism; enriching one's self and philanthropy; getting all the law allows and justice; taking advantage of the other fellow and honesty; becoming engrossed in acquisition and love of family. Now, such contrasts obviously prove nothing more than that money-making is and would be a vicious aim if pursued regardless of these virtues, and it could well be replied that consideration of patriotism, philanthropy, love of family, etc., must in themselves impel one to earn and to save. "The love of money is the root of all evil" implies an exclusive devotion to acquisition that may well be criticized. But aside from this there is no doubt that amid the confused ideas held on the subject, aiming to make money is commonly regarded as in some sort of antagonism to the social virtues.

That there are other sides to the picture is recognized, however, even by the loose thought of the day. The man who earns his living, for instance, it views as one who in so far is performing a fundamental duty. Indeed, the world scorns him who cannot or will not support himself and his family. But this is only to say that one must work to-day to meet the expenditures of to-day. Is this the limit? Is it a virtue for him to work in order to spend, but a vice for him to work in order to save? What are the considerations to be observed by a man in deciding whether or not he should adopt money-making—that is, the acquisition of a surplus beyond his current needs—as one of his definite aims in life?

One consideration relates to our country. The United States is now understood to be spending about $25,000,000 per day in carrying on the war. In the last analysis this amount must be paid out of the past savings and the savings from current earnings of the people of the United States. The wealth of the nation consists mainly of the sum of the wealth of its citizens. We are therefore told to seek increased earnings and to economize in our expenditures in order to enhance the national wealth. The duty here is perfectly clear, but even if we did not have war conditions to teach us as a patriotic responsibility the necessity of earning and saving a surplus, the obligation would still be there. We owe a similar debt to our state and to our city or district. And nearer still comes the duty to one's family and to one's own future, the duty of providing for the rainy day, for old age. And it will be observed that money-making in this sense is directed to the acquisition of net income, it relates to that portion of one's earnings which is saved from current expenditure and becomes capital. Then we must also consider the duty to society. As we look out upon the surrounding evidences of civilization—buildings and railroads and highly cultivated fields, the machinery of production and distribution, the shops full of useful commodities—and then cast our thought backward to a time not very many years ago when all this country was a natural wilderness, we may begin to realize the magnitude of the wealth, the capital, that has come into being since then, every particle of which is due to the earnings and savings of somebody, to the surplus not consumed by the workers of the past, their unexpended and unwasted net balances year by year. Universities, churches, libraries, parks, are included in the wealth thus handed down to us. Our lives to-day may be richer and broader through this inheritance created by the industry and abstinence of our forefathers. Their business careers, now closed, we regard as the more successful in that they earned and saved a surplus, that they had a net income to show as the result of their work.

But these savings of the past were accumulated, after all, by comparatively few of the workers; not by the many, who lived from hand to mouth, happy-go-lucky, spending and enjoying in time of abundance, suffering in time of poverty and stress, making no provision even for their own future, still less recognizing any duty to their country or to posterity to produce economically and regulate their expenditure wisely so as to carry forward a surplus. As far as this majority is concerned we might yet be living among rocks and trees, without shelter, lacking sure supplies of food, with fig leaves to cover our nakedness. And to-day the same conditions obtain. How many persons are to be found among one's acquaintance who feel and act upon any responsibility for doing their "bit" in the creation of capital? Very few. Rather than exert himself to work with this in view, on the one hand, and to abstain from unnecessary consumption, on the other hand, the ordinary man will make to himself every excuse. He will contemn money-making as a sordid aim, readily exaggerating itself into a vice; he will dwell upon the obligations and other considerations of a higher life, this being defined as something generous and noble, a something compared with which money-making cannot be regarded as a worthy object but must be included in the class of unpleasant necessities, not to say indecencies, which ought to be relegated to the background of life; he will summon up pictures of extreme poverty, where any money received must be expended forthwith to meet urgent needs, as justifying that which in his case is the gratification of shiftless indulgence. Above all, this typical individual will not accept and act upon the idea that his affairs, his small income and expenditure, have any bearing upon the prosperity and progress of his country. The most he will keep before him is that he should pay his bills, and perhaps in some few cases, will extend the notion to the future to include provision for the bills and possible emergencies then to be met by himself and his family. Nor is this improvident attitude confined to the young, to the professional and the other non-business classes. In the business world we see it all around us; among those who "work for a living," among clerks and employees and among the so-called laboring classes it appears to be the normal attitude. People who work for salaries or wages seem characteristically to use up all their earnings in their current expenditure, to live up to their incomes without any serious attempt to save. If they pride themselves upon trying to keep out of debt, it is as much as they expect of themselves, and among them the man who attempts to go beyond this in his money affairs is certainly the exception.

One of the effects of a world-wide war is an enormously increased demand for labor at high and advancing wages, a condition that we might suppose would be greatly to the advantage of the laborer. But that will depend upon his own attitude and policy. From England, and from American towns here and there, we hear stories of the wage-earner on whom increasing income has had the effect of lessening the effort to work; who stops during the week when the higher wage scale has paid him the amount he is accustomed to regard as a week's earnings. Now, would it not seem natural to expect that any man encountering improved market conditions for his output, whether of commodity or service, would seek to turn the situation to advantage by increasing that output as largely as lay in his power? If, for instance, I can manufacture shoes to sell for $4.00 a pair and a change in market conditions is such that I can obtain $5.00 a pair, I would endeavor to produce more shoes in order to profit by the favorable market; and if thereafter the price should rise to $6.00 and $7.00 and $8.00 a pair, at each increment my efforts would be still further intensified. That, indeed, is the normal economic attitude. Fluctuations in the price level due to changes in the demand for a commodity are expected to affect, and do affect, the market supply. At a higher price, production is stimulated and more units of the commodity are brought to the market, both from new sources and from old sources. Under falling prices, on the other hand, the supply offered in the market would become automatically diminished.

This is an elementary commonplace in economics, yet the laborer to whom we have just referred does not seem to recognize it. He may find that he can earn in, say four days, an amount equal to his former earnings in six days and, therefore, at the end of the fourth day he quits work for the week. Now, obviously under such increasing wage scale, he might do one of three things:

He could quit at the end of the fourth day, having received a week's income.

He could continue working for the six days and use his surplus earnings for comforts, pleasures, and luxuries which previously he had been unable to afford.

He might work for the six days and save as much as possible of his excess earnings.

Now, what is the wise choice for the laborer? Leaving out of account special cases where he has a large family, or sickness at home, or is under some other disability which in his individual case would reduce his earning power or increase his minimum expenses, ought he not to work for the six days, putting aside all he could of the excess as savings for the future? It will be generally conceded that this is self-evident. If, viewing the narrow conditions under which the workman ordinarily lives, it should be claimed that during a period of unusual earnings self-gratification would be not only natural but measurably justifiable, the reply could be made that this is merely specious, involving assumption not in accord with the facts. Excuses of this kind we often make for ourselves in the endeavor to justify our indulgence in present pleasure rather than perform the irksome duty of self-restraint. The laborer whose ideals are such that he quits at the end of the fourth day is not the type of man who is going to spend the two holidays in pursuing higher aims in life; he is going to pass them in inaction, quite likely at the grog-shop. The man who fails to take advantage of the security for the future offered him and his family through the opportunity of saving from extraordinary earnings is one who is adding to the abnormal demand for such things as phonographs, jewelry, spirits, and tobacco. And this helps to explain the tremendous market for luxuries during wartime. Doubtless there are many workmen who follow a more rational course, who are reaping and storing the harvest for the comfort and security of themselves and their families during the winter of life. Could any one think that this policy involved an aim that was sordid, tending to draw them down, and away from higher considerations of life? Certainly a course of careful planning in one's affairs would be in so far a better course and on a higher plane than indulgence in idleness or shiftless expenditure of surplus for present luxuries, regardless of future need.

This case of the workmen under conditions of abnormal wages seems exceptional; yet the choice so presented to him is not very different fundamentally from the choice normally presented to all the rest of us.

The young man starting out in life may be as negligent of his opportunities as the workman who quits at the end of the fourth day. Or if he devotes himself properly to his vocation he may consume his earnings in current self-gratification. If, however, he will both concentrate on his work and practice self-restraint with the purpose of creating a saved surplus, all will agree in considering him as so far headed on the road towards success. In the case of the beginner this seems clear enough, but, after all, the same considerations apply to everybody else, whether in business or profession, beginners or experienced, young or old; to all of us is the same choice presented daily, and at our peril we must make it wisely. The physician, for instance, although he cannot afford to pay more attention to money-making than to the welfare of his patients, to his studies, to his professional ideals, must not, on the other hand, leave out of account these business duties and considerations which belong to him as an economic member of society. He must produce and must consume with his family, reasonably, decently and thriftily. He must aim at a surplus to store away for the future. These aims are, as a matter of course, secondary to his professional ideals, but there need be no conflict of duty. The point is that there exists a department of his activity devoted, and to be devoted, by him to his business affairs. In any event, as a man, a husband, a father, a citizen, he cannot escape from the responsibility of these business affairs. They must be conducted in some way. Shall it be well or ill? If he fails herein it may involve failure in any or all these relations— as a man, husband, father, citizen. And obviously these same considerations apply to all other men and women, whatever may be their professions, occupations, or major interests in life. Why do so many allow themselves to be dragged along, living from hand-to-mouth, in fear of the knock of the bill collector at the door? Why do we associate money questions with that which is unhappy, unfortunate, down-at-the-heel, with fear and misery? Barring mere accidents, it is because we are careless, shiftless; because we do not face the problem manfully, practice reasonable self-restraint, consider the subject in its complexity and decide upon, and carry out, a constructive programme. Even if one happens to possess wealth, he is not exempt. Indeed, large wealth involves still greater necessity for care in the conduct of one's pecuniary affairs. The rich man is said to have perplexities and responsibilities which are unknown to those in moderate circumstances. In fine, everyone must face these money questions or be driven by them.

Those who live on fixed incomes, whether from salary or investment, may find it impossible to make any direct attempt to make money; for them the problem is to be confronted and mastered on its other side, the side of spending and saving, that the income may be apportioned as wisely as possible for the purposes of living. But during the last few years a new factor has entered into the money problems of the individual, often adding to his trials, often adding to his self-made excuses, and especially burdensome to the man on fixed income. We refer to the high cost of living. Here it is, however, that the wage earner can do something in self-protection, for the level of prices may be in some measure affected by his policy in handling his earnings.

A period of high wages is accompanied by and is in some sense an incident of a high level of prices. Now we recognize high wages, considered in itself, as beneficial to the community, for it gives opportunity, at least, for comforts in life and a provision for the future that otherwise would be lacking. But if prices have advanced as much as wages, the apparent improvement to the laborer is merely in nominal wages, while that which alone can benefit him is higher real wages. Now let us see what the workman could do to advance real wages as contrasted with nominal wages.

What will be the effect on prices of the use of surplus earnings during a period of high wages?

If the surplus earnings are expended, they will be used either in meeting the higher prices of customary commodities, or in meeting these advanced prices and also in purchasing additional commodities. The first case will occur only if, and when, the advance in price equals the advance in wages, for only in that event will the new wages just cover the new cost of customary commodities. Then this expenditure of the entire income in customary commodities tends to keep up the price level and any benefit from higher wages disappears.

In the second case, so far as the worker spends his surplus earnings in meeting advanced prices for customary commodities, he tends to maintain prices at the higher level, and so far as he buys additional commodities, he increases the demand for them and tends further to advance the price level.

If, on the other hand, the worker will save from his surplus earnings, he will increase the community's capital, and this will tend, directly or indirectly, to cause the production of further commodities, so increasing the supply of commodities and therefore tending to reduce prices.

In any case, the worker should save as much as possible, as this tends to reduce the price level and so to better his condition. Or, putting it more simply, in time of high wages the worker ought to produce as much as possible and consume as little as possible, both influences tending to increase the stock of commodities for his ultimate gain and for that of the community.

In fact, a high level of prices may be due measurably to some wasting of the world's capital—as in war, for instance—and then the only antidote is to restore the capital, a movement that would doubtless occur anyway in time but which could be greatly accelerated through a general adoption of habits of thrift and saving throughout a community.

This then, though small, is something definite that we can contribute to the material advancement of mankind and, like the duty in this connection to our nation, to our families and ourselves, it consists in creating capital; that is, earning as much as we can and, in any event, even if our earnings are fixed, managing the income thriftily, and carrying forward as large a net result as possible.

We turn now from the mass of mankind, on the whole so singularly neglectful of these responsibilities, to the few in number who constitute the creators of capital, to whom are due so much of the comforts, the conveniences, and the material advantages that go to make civilized life possible. Now these few are found in every rank in life. They may be rich or poor, professional or business men, employer or employee, old or young, male or female. The characteristic is their habit of thrift, of definitely adopting money-making as an aim, of spending less than they earn. It is astonishing what a small percentage of mankind they are. The Income Tax returns in the United States for 1916 showed that out of a population of 104,000,000 people those with taxable incomes aggregated only 336,652, about one in three hundred. But whatever be the rank of the individual practicing this thrift he is headed in the right direction and he tends to reach the point of relative competence, of independence in his pecuniary affairs.

Preëminent in the class of the thrifty we think of the man of affairs; the business enterprise indeed is supposed to be the money-maker, par excellence. Money-making is in fact considered as its raison d'être; it is as a money-maker that the business man is contemned by some and envied by many.

Now money-making and money values occupy a special place in business enterprise, due to the fact that on economic principles such money value becomes the best test—perhaps the only true test—of the workableness and success of business efforts. In the complicated activities of the world's work, where each man, each undertaking, each business unit, respectively, is striving primarily for its own advantage, how is it, among all this pulling and pushing, this competition, that the social income is distributed so nearly in accordance with the individual contribution? Even if we admit that many persons fail to get a fair share, that there is gross inequality here and there, still after all, a student of mankind's activities in production, distribution, and consumption must marvel at the extent to which the rewards approximate the value of contribution. Now this is made possible by money considered as a measure of relative values, by the standard or test of fitness embodied in the thought, Will it pay, and to what extent will it pay? If I have in mind some new invention that will perhaps confer benefits on mankind, the best test of its practicability and utility will be, Will it pay, will people buy it, pay money for it? If an improvement in process is proposed, the question is, Will it pay? If the young man starts out in life with high ideals and a reasonably good opinion of his own abilities, an opinion fostered perhaps by fond parents and admiring friends, the question is, Will these abilities fit in with the world's needs? Will they supply a real demand, will they be serviceable? The best means of ascertaining this, although it may be only a rough estimate and although errors occasionally creep in is, will they pay? Can he sell these services for real money? This criterion is practically omnipresent in the world of affairs. It is based on economic necessity, and although here and there it may be charged with cruelties, with serious blunders, it is, on the whole, a remarkably accurate standard. We see this more clearly where we attempt to substitute some other criterion for ranking the soldiers in the battle of life. We can note, for instance, the inferior type and character, generally speaking, of men elected to office by the suffrages of their fellow citizens, compared with men who reach positions of authority in business and other enterprises through the pressure of these economic principles. Again, consider the nation that has attempted to improve on economic distribution of power by evolving a government which places the power in the hands of those best fitted to govern, a ruling class which aims directly at efficiency, a select class but necessarily self-selected, thus supplanting an economic régime by a military régime—successful truly in certain forms of economic efficiency through a more rigid and compact organization, but destructive of the initiative, the evolutionary growth, the fundamental development, the liberties of the people. Contrast this with the freedom, happiness, and progress of a nation of shop-keepers. Now this economic régime, with its individual instances of cruelty, like the cruelties of nature, does on the whole tend to develop men, to require their best efforts, to make them come forward and upward. Thus, in this interplay of economic forces, wealth, or money, or profits stands out as a primary object of attainment, and becomes the incentive to the complex efforts which tend to benefit the individual, the community, and the nation.

The business enterprise then directs its attention to profits, because, from mere economic necessity, profits are the criterion of the true success of the enterprise, that is, its serviceability to mankind. Here we distinguish between the shortsighted man, who aims at immediate returns, and the farsighted man, whose eye is fixed on the future, who verily desires the profits, but desires them in the long run. But this is only a manifestation of human nature as we find it in every field. We always note a deficiency in the man whose life is lived for the present, for immediate enjoyment: in him we see the typical pleasure-seeker, peculiarly prone to temptation, to break the rules of life, to indulge himself at the expense of others or of his own future. He is characteristically the weakling, the wrongdoer. And we contrast him with the man of character, who stands superior to an immediate environment, who will not disregard the distant future, the absent neighbor, the invisible God. And so in the economic world it is the whole life period which is to be regarded when aims are chosen. Profits as a goal for the long run do not antagonize moral principles. "Honesty is the best policy" and "Do unto others as you would have others do unto you" are maxims of good business; and that economic principles do not conflict with them is shown by the fact that they tend towards profits in the long run. This is not to assert that mankind in business is perfect. In every period of economic advance into a new environment, men try new experiments, as during the development of the great modern corporation in the period following the Civil War in this country and, earlier than that, in the era of railroad building. They have tried new experiments in ethics as they have in physics, in chemistry, in economics. They have attempted to replace honesty by camouflage, the golden rule by self-aggrandizement. But these attempts are not successful and so they become discredited; they do not work because inherently they cannot last, and inability to endure is fatal to the purposes of any economic undertaking. We are emphasizing the fact that business is necessarily conducted for the long run, the very nature of success implying permanence. A man may take some criminal advantage of an opportunity: he may abscond with money entrusted to him; he may abuse the confidence reposed in him by an employer, by a customer; he may obtain an immediate profit by misrepresentation. But no one could expect such things to last; he could not possibly be building an enduring structure; such a course could not in the end promise him profits, or any other kind of success. A properly conducted business enterprise then is concerned with making profits in the long run; that is to say, in accordance with accepted notions of business conduct; in short, according to rules of the game, and this involves conformity with a standard, a standard of giving good value for what one gets.

We must next distinguish between gross profits and net profits. The merchant or manufacturer naturally desires to do a large business, he points with pride to the increase in his sales this year over last year. The larger his turnover the smaller the proportionate amount of his overhead expenses that must be borne per unit of product, and other economies follow large-scale production or distribution. He may occasionally be desirous of increasing his output even when it entails a disproportionate increase in his expenditures, with the idea that he can later occupy himself with reducing these expenses and in the meanwhile the goodwill of his enterprise will have gained from the larger circle of customers. Such is the case with a new enterprise that often starts out with the expectation of little or no profits during its early years, when it is gathering a clientèle and learning to distribute its product with economy. All these, however, are special cases. The normal situation is that the business enterprise is aiming at net profits, having an interest in large sales, heavy transactions and gross profits only so far as these are expected to lead finally to net profits, the real goal. Now these net profits are, of course, the remainder of earnings left on hand after providing for all costs and expenses, for depreciation and every other factor causing loss, destruction, and deterioration during the business period under consideration. In short, the business capital as it was at the beginning of the period is first fully restored and made intact at the end of the period before a net profit emerges. This net profit therefore becomes in a true sense a creation of new capital and may indeed be retained in the business as an addition to capital funds. Even when it is paid out in dividends, partly or wholly, it becomes new capital in the hands of the individual stockholders who then in their private capacity may of course spend it, but by proper investment may keep it permanently stored as capital. It is the creation of capital then, that is in reality the ultimate money-making aim of the business enterprise.

We can now summarize the attitude and policy of the typical business man in his money-making aim as follows:

In seeking profits he is actuated by economic necessity.

His goal is profits in the long run, which involves conformity with economic and ethical standards, and net profits, which implies the creation of capital.

The creation of capital we cannot fail to recognize as a worthy aim. It has given mankind much of all that mankind possesses and constitutes the foundation upon which civilization largely rests. The advancement in the arts and sciences has been in no small degree stimulated by the demands of business enterprise for new methods of creating capital and we may believe that should the time arrive when this motive should fail, when men should grow to be indifferent in their attitude towards profits, the ensuing stagnation would affect every department of human endeavor. Of this we may be assured even when we remember that money-making, and what goes with it, is not the only aim in life.

After cataloguing so much that is virtuous in the pursuit of money-making the suggestion is inevitable that there must be some other side to it, that the common views of the rapacity of the money-maker cannot be wholly unfounded. What then are the vices of the money-making aim? In examining this question we shall first brush aside some things to which we have already referred. The pathological cases of mere crime, of sharp practice, of taking advantage of others, while mounting up into distressingly high figures considered absolutely, are much less important relatively; that is, they are infrequent and scarce enough to avoid obscuring the rule which they violate, the rule that honesty is indispensable in economics as well as in ethics. What we must now investigate is any vicious tendencies that may be found in the money-making aim when followed normally and according to its own accepted principles. Of such degenerative tendencies we seem to find two: first, the tendency to that excess which becomes a vice; and second, the tendency to a disregard of other considerations in life through too exclusive a devotion to acquisitiveness. But upon further thought we must see that these two tendencies flow together and become one, for too much devotion to money-getting and too little attention to the other purposes of life are, after all, expressions of the same thing. Perhaps a man may err in excessive devotion to any object of life but we must admit that in the pursuit of gain the evil tendency to exaggerated absorption in the one aim is promoted through a coöperation with his natural selfishness. Of all the fields of human endeavor, here is one that peculiarly fits in with self-seeking, with disregard for others, which may drag a man downward, making him small and mean, unhappy and uncharitable, while apparently attaining the goal at which he has aimed. Not every man, while concentrating upon money-making, is consciously seeking his country's welfare, the amelioration of life for the many, the uplift of posterity, even if he rigidly adheres to the accepted rules of the game, to the code of business honor. This brings us back to the popular picture of the money-maker, grasping, sordid, narrow-minded. There are such people. I believe them to be rare, but whether there are many of them to-day or not, it is a type tending to disappear in the environment of modern business which offers its inducements and rewards to him who does, who becomes, who renders service, not to the sordid seeker for gain. Barring an occasional exception, such an exclusive aim is not that of the man of large affairs, the business leader, the conspicuously successful man. It is not Harriman, nor Edison, nor Weinstock, nor Marshall Field, nor Peabody, nor is it the heads of our big corporations of to-day. Such men are money-makers, creators of capital, builders of large enterprise, but their aim at profits while genuine is only incidental to their main purpose of doing, of becoming better able to achieve, of rendering service. When the beginner in business approaches an experienced friend for advice, he is told to work as hard and as faithfully as possible, to study his business, to seek to improve himself—in other words, to concentrate his whole strength on the giving of service, for his wages or salary will take care of itself. The experienced man knows well that this holds just as truly for all ranks in the business world and that the higher one ascends in responsibilities, the more he must give and do; indeed the leading positions in the business world are occupied by men who produce tremendously, whose value to themselves and others lies in what they accomplish, and this—not what they get—is the criterion of success among men of experience, among those in charge of enterprises, who are on the lookout for leaders of this type.

Here we have the remedy for the tendency backed by natural selfishness towards undue devotion to gain: such narrowness simply does not work, it is crowded out by competition with the superior efficiency of broader motives. And while, here and there, the type continues to exist, its development in new cases is discouraged by every instance illustrating the relative success—in all senses— attained by those who make it their chief aim to produce, to render service. Just as the physician bestows his first thought upon his patient, these superior business men give first consideration to their profession, for so they regard it, and this tends to assure their success, just as it does that of the physician, and to become the standardized ideal for lesser men.

It is indeed clearly self-evident that on many accounts the man in business must give attention primarily to the service he is trying to render. The clerk in the store must devote himself mainly to his customers, to his merchandise, to his other duties, not to his salary. And so with the department manager, and so with the general manager, whether of a store, a railroad company, or other activity; the immediate daily problem for all lies in the rendering of a service, the producing of a commodity, or the doing of the thing for which the business enterprise exists. This concentration upon output is furthermore required by competition which whips the producer into line and often makes it a matter of business life and death that one should make progress in method and quality. That his shoes wear is a matter of pride to the shoe manufacturer. "Blank tires are good tires" is not to be regarded as merely a boastful advertisement. If it was it would not pay the advertising cost.

Money-making as an aim thus becomes subsidiary to the characteristic activities of the enterprise, it is in a sense a by-product. But the money-making aim is there, although perhaps in the background. It is furnishing the power under which the enterprise operates. More than that, it is the gauge indicating the prosperity or lack of prosperity of the enterprise, its progress, its fitting in with the needs of life. In short, the money-making aim spurs on the business enterprise, just as the weekly or monthly pay spurs on the humble worker; but in each case the main attention is given, and necessarily given, to the work to be performed.

Let us now consider some of the implications of this concentration on rendering service. The directed effort of each man to the production of the utility characteristic of his business, tends to result in his learning to conduct that specific activity with a high degree of skill, and with an increasingly valuable fund of experience. So highly specialized does he become that it will be quite impossible for any one hitherto a stranger in that sphere to conduct it as well. Therefore in an age of coördinated effort the more a man has of accumulated knowledge and facility in handling a certain kind of affair and the better fitted, therefore, he is to continue and to progress along that line, the less relatively he is able to undertake the affairs of some other kind with which he is not familiar. We commonly feel free to criticize a railroad, a newspaper, a large business house, perhaps a university, with which we may have casual contact, but the fact is there are few competent critics outside of the ranks of the enterprise itself or of those carrying on activities that are directly similar. In a word, through this focusing of attention, a man will come to be exhaustively familiar with his own occupation, while possessing a merely superficial acquaintance with the theories, customs, and responsibilities of those of others. The wise man therefore argues the necessity of confining himself to the field in which he has become expert and will avoid taking chances in some outside direction wherein he is not familiar. One of the most common and disheartening experiences in the money-making and money-saving of the thrifty is that after having both worked hard and practiced self-restraint, the resultant savings are often put into some enterprise that turns out badly, and the whole effort is thus thrown away. Generally this happens because he has violated the rule we have just stated; he has ventured his savings in unfamiliar fields, ignorantly he has rushed in where the better informed would have feared to tread. Such so-called investments are in reality highly speculative. They involve risks which are unknown and altogether to be avoided. Now no one speculates in his own legitimate business, for there he is acquainted with the hazards which, he has learned, require the best of knowledge and the greatest of prudence. It is the allurement of the unknown that tempts him to seek unearned profits through speculation in outside regions where, in the nature of the case, the chances must be against him. Now speculation has its proper place in business: there are certain inherent hazards that must be undertaken, mainly to be found in the risk of the seasons in the production of crops, and the risk of the future in undeveloped enterprise. These risks must be carried by somebody, but clearly they constitute an activity for specialists who study conditions, becoming relatively expert in determining how and when to act. These specialists are drawn principally from two classes: First, the professional speculator, who knows his markets and makes a business of buying and selling future risks; such men perform a great service in handling our seasonal crops and in other directions, and are entitled to a reasonable profit. Second, the man of wealth who may use part of his surplus in the risks of undeveloped enterprise; although it is probable that in the end his losses and expenses will outweigh his gains, he can afford to take chances of such experiments in the hope that success will follow in some of them; furthermore, he can regard the outlay as a contribution to the advancement of mankind. For the rest of us, however, outside of these two classes, it is our business to keep away from speculation whether in oil wells, flying machines, in new factories, or in real estate: in the long run, we cannot get something for nothing and money-making efforts that are ethically valid thus coincide with those that are selfishly desirable, namely, the efforts to obtain the payment, the profit, that arises from a valuable service performed or commodity produced. Too often men who follow this rule in their regular occupation depart from it in the use of their saved surplus funds. They feel that their savings ought to make them money, as they say.

Now savings can be employed in one of three ways: They may be used as capital by the owner; or they may be put out in investments—that is, used or utilized as capital in the business of another; or, third, they may be wasted in gambling or speculation. As a matter of course, the employment as additional capital in one's own enterprise is generally the most desirable wherever applicable, but this is a use of limited scope, relating to but few of the people engaged in productive activity who earn and save a surplus. The main resource for such accumulations is in safe investments, in the bonds and securities of our own country and those of well established enterprises. Not many among our embryo capitalists possess the experience or skill requisite for the safe and proper investment of their funds, they must rely upon the advice of others. But whom can they trust? The demand for investment advice has not failed to call forth a supply of advisers, and elaborate are the schemes designed to lure the unwary. But, generally speaking, the man who falls into the clutches of these birds of prey has himself to blame, for the reason that the temptations they offer are appeals to the illegitimate desire to get something for nothing or to the foolish notion that one can get-rich-quick in some way whispered about by a stranger, and out of sheer benevolence. The fact is that the wise man will dismiss all thought of making money out of his investments; he will seek only the moderate return which alone is consistent with safety; and with this policy, will turn a deaf ear to any so-called opportunity which promises big profits. We can summarize the matter by saying that concentration upon one's business and service implies that one should not attempt to make money elsewhere.

This concentration on one's affairs therefore grows

into a sort of practical system in which each member of the business community is looking after some function or activity to the exclusion of other things. And so the world's work is carried on to the best advantage, each function being filled by those particular men who have become relatively expert therein. From this system arises a business habit or method not always understood by the young and inexperienced, by the non-business person. We refer to the practice in trade of leaving to each individual, to each enterprise, to each organization, the responsibility for looking out for its own interests when having dealings with others. Caveat emptor—let the buyer beware—expresses an extreme development of this, and in its common signification, that each side is to be permitted and expected to take any advantage of the other side that it may be able to secure, it describes a state of warfare rather than of business. In buying and selling, in aiming to obtain the most favorable terms for each line of his activity, in meeting conditions of competition, in all these relations, the business man is endeavoring to better himself and may doubtless be tempted here and there to forget the interests of the other party to the transaction. But to yield to such temptation would merely be to abuse a principle which on the whole is sanctioned by the requirements of economic efficiency. This principle is that the nearest approximation to effective justice in business transactions is reached when on each side the parties devote themselves to their respective interests and points of view. If A has a house for sale and B is a prospective buyer, the essence of the possible transaction between the two is that A's idea of the value of the property is different from B's idea of that value; or at any rate that A sees less value in it to him than does B to B. This is of course typical of all business transactions—the seller desires the money above the commodity, the buyer prefers the commodity to the money. The seller and the buyer each dwells naturally upon his own idea of value. This is altogether desirable, not to say indispensable, and is characteristic of every relation of business, wherever two men buy and sell, employ one another, or have other dealings together. The situation is somewhat the same as in a law suit where the duty of the attorney for the plaintiff is to make every point that fairly can be made for the plaintiff, while the attorney on the other side must correspondingly make every point that can properly be made for the defendant. Each side is supposed to look after the interest of that side. Similarly, in a business organization, say a railroad, when some new project is under consideration it will be submitted to the engineer, to the chemist, to the attorney, to the practical transportation man, and in each of these departments it is expected that the wisdom born of experience in the particular function will be brought to bear. The engineer speaks with authority on engineering questions, the lawyer on legal questions, the transportation man on the practical working out of the project; and, normally, the criticisms and contribution of each are confined to his own function. In short, the régime of economic self-interest results in leaving to each the responsibility which he is most competent to assume, that in which he is most expert, which thereby receives the best attention that generally speaking it could have. Nor are correctives lacking for the abuses which may enter in through an overdevelopment of self-interest. Caveat emptor becomes discredited as an unmodified basis of human action. The golden rule is increasingly seen to constitute a foundation demanded by economics as well as by ethics. The trend to-day is away from indifference to the interests of those with whom we deal. The successful merchant will not attempt to make a profit through sales which he knows would not benefit the purchaser, for that would not measure up to the test, Will it pay? The value of a business depends largely on its goodwill and too much money and effort are spent in advertising and other means of building up a clientèle to make men conceive it to be to their interest to deal sharply with their customers.

In the efforts of scientists to seek out and establish new methods, new principles, the success of an experiment is to be determined, I suppose, by the test, Will it work? Does it yield effective results? Similarly, in economics, the science of mankind in its production, distribution and consumption of material things, the test of utility and efficiency is, Will it pay? that being the standard of workableness in the application of that science.

We have attempted, therefore, in this analysis of money-making to apply this test, because the practice or habit or influence that pays is that which is in accord so far with the principles underlying this branch of social science. We have seen, according to this standard, that it is the duty of all to adopt money-making as a conscious aim; that the money is to be economically used, the final object being net profit, that balance or remainder which is carried forward as created capital. Inability to increase a fixed income does not absolve one from the duty of doing one's part in the creation of capital through thrift and saving. The business enterprise, moreover, is required by economic necessity to aim at money-making—meaning, however, profits in the long run rather than immediate or temporary gains. Such permanent returns can only be sought through adherence to ethical principles and although this aim at profits becomes the power plant which drives the business machine, the latter gives its energies and attention more directly to the rendering of service.

Concentration upon service tends to make a man relatively efficient therein, but argues a relative unfamiliarity with the field of others, from which we infer the advisability of confining one's activity to the thing he has learned to do best. As an example of this, he should avoid placing his surplus capital or savings in outside enterprises where they will partake of risks that are unknown to him, nor should he attempt to employ his savings at all with the purpose of making money, unless, indeed, he can use them as capital in his own business. The focusing of attention on one's own function also implies and explains the custom of placing upon participants in a business transaction the responsibility each for his own side, a custom which is economically justified but which must be kept within proper limits, as is fully recognized by the business men who are successful and who therefore become models or examples for the guidance of other men, influencing the latter towards high ideals.

We have found, on the other hand, that apart from men in charge of business enterprise, the burden of providing thus for man's welfare and development is assumed by very few, the vast majority, whether in professional or business employment, treating it with neglect and contempt. They think, perhaps, that they are aiming at higher things, or that their efforts would not sufficiently count, or they do not give the matter any sturdy thought; while the underlying motive, often unconscious, is simply an unwillingness to practice self-restraint. It is self-indulgence, we must conclude, that is to be overcome if we are to meet this responsibility in a manly way, visualizing it with sufficient clearness to see that thrift, the creation of capital for one's self and for the race, comes into no necessary conflict with any other proper aim in life, but on the contrary constitutes a fundamental duty to society, to the state, to one's family, to his own future, to his self-respect.

CHAPTER IX.

MEN OF BUSINESS.

"Seest thou a man diligent in his business? he shall stand before kings."—Proverbs of Solomon.

"That man is but of the lower part of the world that is

137

not brought up to business and affairs."—Owen Feltham.

HAZLITT, in one of his clever essays, represents the man of business as a mean sort of person put in a go-cart, yoked to a trade or profession; alleging that all he has to do is, not to go out of the beaten track, but merely to let his affairs take their own course. "The great requisite," he says, "for the prosperous management of ordinary business is the want of imagination, or of any ideas but those of custom and interest on the narrowest scale." [263] But nothing could be more one-sided, and in effect untrue, than such a definition. Of course, there are narrow-minded men of business, as there are narrow-minded scientific men, literary men, and legislators; but there are also business men of large and comprehensive minds, capable of action on the very largest scale. As Burke said in his speech on the India Bill, he knew statesmen who were pedlers, and merchants who acted in the spirit of statesmen.

If we take into account the qualities necessary for the successful conduct of any important undertaking,—that it requires special aptitude, promptitude of action on emergencies, capacity for organizing the labours often of large numbers of men, great tact and knowledge of human nature, constant self-culture, and growing experience in the practical affairs of life,—it must, we think, be obvious that the school of business is by no means so narrow as some writers would have us believe. Mr. Helps had gone much nearer the truth when he said that consummate men of business are as rare almost as great poets,—rarer, perhaps, than veritable saints and martyrs. Indeed, of no other pursuit can it so emphatically be said, as of this, that "Business makes men."

It has, however, been a favourite fallacy with dunces in all times, that men of genius are unfitted for business, as well as that business occupations unfit men for the pursuits of genius. The unhappy youth who committed suicide a few years since because he had been "born to be a man and condemned to be a grocer," proved by the act that his soul was not equal even to the dignity of grocery. For it is not the calling that degrades the man, but the man that degrades the calling. All work that brings honest gain is honourable, whether it be of hand or mind. The fingers may be soiled, yet the heart remain pure; for it is not material so much as moral dirt that defiles—greed far more than grime, and vice than verdigris.

The greatest have not disdained to labour honestly and usefully for a living, though at the same time aiming after higher things. Thales, the first of the seven sages, Solon, the second founder of Athens, and Hyperates, the mathematician, were all traders. Plato, called the Divine by reason of the excellence of his wisdom, defrayed his travelling expenses in Egypt by the profits derived from the oil which he sold during his journey. Spinoza maintained himself by polishing glasses while he pursued his philosophical investigations. Linnæus, the great botanist, prosecuted his studies while hammering leather and making shoes. Shakespeare was a successful manager of a theatre—perhaps priding himself more upon his practical qualities in that capacity than on his writing of plays and poetry. Pope was of opinion that Shakespeare's principal object in cultivating literature was to secure an honest independence. Indeed he seems to have been altogether indifferent to literary reputation. It is not known that he superintended the publication of a single play, or even sanctioned the printing of one; and the chronology of his writings is still a mystery. It is certain, however, that he prospered in his business, and realized sufficient to enable him to retire upon a competency to his native town of Stratford-upon-Avon.

Chaucer was in early life a soldier, and afterwards an effective Commissioner of Customs, and Inspector of Woods and Crown Lands. Spencer was Secretary to the Lord Deputy of Ireland, was afterwards Sheriff of Cork, and is said to have been shrewd and attentive in matters of business. Milton, originally a schoolmaster, was elevated to the post of Secretary to the Council of State during the Commonwealth; and the extant Order-book of the Council, as well as many of Milton's letters which are preserved, give abundant evidence of his activity and usefulness in that office. Sir Isaac Newton proved himself an efficient Master of the Mint; the new coinage of 1694 having been carried on under his immediate personal superintendence. Cowper prided himself upon his business punctuality, though he confessed that he "never knew a poet, except himself, who was punctual in anything." But against this we may set the lives of Wordsworth and Scott—the former a distributor of stamps, the latter a clerk to the Court of Session,—both of whom, though great poets, were eminently punctual and practical men of business. David Ricardo, amidst the occupations of his daily business as a London stock-jobber, in conducting which he acquired an ample fortune, was able to concentrate his mind upon his favourite subject—on which he was enabled to throw great light— the principles of political economy; for he united in himself the sagacious commercial man and the profound philosopher. Baily, the eminent astronomer, was another stockbroker; and Allen, the chemist, was a silk manufacturer.

We have abundant illustrations, in our own day, of the fact that the highest intellectual power is not incompatible with the active and efficient performance of routine duties. Grote, the great historian of Greece, was a London banker. And it is not long since John Stuart Mill, one of our greatest living thinkers, retired from the Examiner's department of the East India Company, carrying with him the admiration and esteem of his fellow officers, not on account of his high views of philosophy, but because of the high standard of efficiency which he had established in his office, and the thoroughly satisfactory manner in which he had conducted the business of his department.

The path of success in business is usually the path of common sense. Patient labour and application are as necessary here as in the acquisition of knowledge or the pursuit of science. The old Greeks said, "to become an able man in any profession, three things are necessary— nature, study, and practice." In business, practice, wisely and diligently improved, is the great secret of success. Some may make what are called "lucky hits," but like money earned by gambling, such "hits" may only serve to lure one to ruin. Bacon was accustomed to say that it was in business as in ways—the nearest way was commonly the foulest, and that if a man would go the fairest way he must go somewhat about. The journey may occupy a longer time, but the pleasure of the labour involved by it, and the enjoyment of the results produced, will be more genuine and unalloyed. To have a daily appointed task of even common drudgery to do makes the rest of life feel all the sweeter.

The fable of the labours of Hercules is the type of all human doing and success. Every youth should be made to feel that his happiness and well-doing in life must necessarily rely mainly on himself and the exercise of his own energies, rather than upon the help and patronage of others. The late Lord Melbourne embodied a piece of useful advice in a letter which he wrote to Lord John Russell, in reply to an application for a provision for one of Moore the poet's sons: "My dear John," he said, "I return you Moore's letter. I shall be ready to do what you like about it when we have the means. I think whatever is done should be done for Moore himself. This is more distinct, direct, and intelligible. Making a small provision for young men is hardly justifiable; and it is of all things the most prejudicial to themselves. They think what they have much larger than it really is; and they make no exertion. The young should never hear any language but this: 'You have your own way to make, and it depends upon your own exertions whether you starve or not.'

Believe me, &c., MELBOURNE."

Practical industry, wisely and vigorously applied, always produces its due effects. It carries a man onward, brings out his individual character, and stimulates the action of others. All may not rise equally, yet each, on the whole, very much according to his deserts. "Though all cannot live on the piazza," as the Tuscan proverb has it, "every one may feel the sun."

On the whole, it is not good that human nature should have the road of life made too easy. Better to be under the necessity of working hard and faring meanly, than to have everything done ready to our hand and a pillow of down to repose upon. Indeed, to start in life with comparatively small means seems so necessary as a stimulus to work, that it may almost be set down as one of the conditions essential to success in life. Hence, an eminent judge, when asked what contributed most to success at the bar, replied, "Some succeed by great talent, some by high connexions, some by miracle, but the majority by commencing without a shilling."

We have heard of an architect of considerable accomplishments,—a man who had improved himself by long study, and travel in the classical lands of the East,— who came home to commence the practice of his profession. He determined to begin anywhere, provided he could be employed; and he accordingly undertook a business connected with dilapidations,—one of the lowest and least remunerative departments of the architect's calling. But he had the good sense not to be above his trade, and he had the resolution to work his way upward, so that he only got a fair start. One hot day in July a friend found him sitting astride of a house roof occupied with his dilapidation business. Drawing his hand across his perspiring countenance, he exclaimed, "Here's a pretty business for a man who has been all over Greece!" However, he did his work, such as it was, thoroughly and well; he persevered until he advanced by degrees to more remunerative branches of employment, and eventually he rose to the highest walks of his profession.

The necessity of labour may, indeed, be regarded as the main root and spring of all that we call progress in individuals, and civilization in nations; and it is doubtful whether any heavier curse could be imposed on man than the complete gratification of all his wishes without effort on his part, leaving nothing for his hopes, desires or struggles. The feeling that life is destitute of any motive or necessity for action, must be of all others the most distressing and insupportable to a rational being. The Marquis de Spinola asking Sir Horace Vere what his brother died of, Sir Horace replied, "He died, Sir, of having nothing to do." "Alas!" said Spinola, "that is enough to kill any general of us all."

Those who fail in life are however very apt to assume a tone of injured innocence, and conclude too hastily that everybody excepting themselves has had a hand in their personal misfortunes. An eminent writer lately published a book, in which he described his numerous failures in business, naively admitting, at the same time, that he was ignorant of the multiplication table; and he came to the conclusion that the real cause of his ill-success in life was the money-worshipping spirit of the age. Lamartine also did not hesitate to profess his contempt for arithmetic; but, had it been less, probably we should not have witnessed the unseemly spectacle of the admirers of that distinguished personage engaged in collecting subscriptions for his support in his old age.

Again, some consider themselves born to ill luck, and make up their minds that the world invariably goes against them without any fault on their own part. We have heard of a person of this sort, who went so far as to declare his belief that if he had been a hatter people would have been born without heads! There is however a Russian proverb which says that Misfortune is next door to Stupidity; and it will often be found that men who are constantly lamenting their luck, are in some way or other reaping the consequences of their own neglect, mismanagement, improvidence, or want of application. Dr. Johnson, who came up to London with a single guinea in his pocket, and who once accurately described himself in his signature to a letter addressed to a noble lord, as Impransus, or Dinnerless, has honestly said, "All the complaints which are made of the world are unjust; I never knew a man of merit neglected; it was generally by his own fault that he failed of success."

Washington Irving, the American author, held like views. "As for the talk," said he, "about modest merit being neglected, it is too often a cant, by which indolent and irresolute men seek to lay their want of success at the door of the public. Modest merit is, however, too apt to be inactive, or negligent, or uninstructed merit. Well matured and well disciplined talent is always sure of a market, provided it exerts itself; but it must not cower at home and expect to be sought for. There is a good deal of cant too about the success of forward and impudent men, while men of retiring worth are passed over with neglect. But it usually happens that those forward men have that valuable quality of promptness and activity without which worth is a mere inoperative property. A barking dog is often more useful than a sleeping lion."

Attention, application, accuracy, method, punctuality, and despatch, are the principal qualities required for the efficient conduct of business of any sort. These, at first sight, may appear to be small matters; and yet they are of essential importance to human happiness, well-being, and usefulness. They are little things, it is true; but human life is made up of comparative trifles. It is the repetition of little acts which constitute not only the sum of human character, but which determine the character of nations. And where men or nations have broken down, it will almost invariably be found that neglect of little things was the rock on which they split. Every human being has duties to be performed, and, therefore, has need of cultivating the capacity for doing them; whether the sphere of action be the management of a household, the conduct of a trade or profession, or the government of a nation.

The examples we have already given of great workers in various branches of industry, art, and science, render it unnecessary further to enforce the importance of persevering application in any department of life. It is the result of every-day experience that steady attention to matters of detail lies at the root of human progress; and that diligence, above all, is the mother of good luck. Accuracy is also of much importance, and an invariable mark of good training in a man. Accuracy in observation, accuracy in speech, accuracy in the transaction of affairs. What is done in business must be well done; for it is better to accomplish perfectly a small amount of work, than to half-do ten times as much. A wise man used to say, "Stay a little, that we may make an end the sooner."

Too little attention, however, is paid to this highly important quality of accuracy. As a man eminent in practical science lately observed to us, "It is astonishing how few people I have met with in the course of my experience, who can define a fact accurately." Yet in business affairs, it is the manner in which even small matters are transacted, that often decides men for or against you. With virtue, capacity, and good conduct in other respects, the person who is habitually inaccurate cannot be trusted; his work has to be gone over again; and he thus causes an infinity of annoyance, vexation, and trouble.

It was one of the characteristic qualities of Charles James Fox, that he was thoroughly pains-taking in all that he did. When appointed Secretary of State, being piqued at some observation as to his bad writing, he actually took a writing-master, and wrote copies like a schoolboy until he had sufficiently improved himself. Though a corpulent man, he was wonderfully active at picking up cut tennis balls, and when asked how he contrived to do so, he playfully replied, "Because I am a very pains-taking man." The same accuracy in trifling matters was displayed by him in things of greater importance; and he acquired his reputation, like the painter, by "neglecting nothing."

Method is essential, and enables a larger amount of work to be got through with satisfaction. "Method," said the Reverend Richard Cecil, "is like packing things in a box; a good packer will get in half as much again as a bad one." Cecil's despatch of business was extraordinary, his maxim being, "The shortest way to do many things is to do only one thing at once;" and he never left a thing undone with a view of recurring to it at a period of more leisure. When business pressed, he rather chose to encroach on his hours of meals and rest than omit any part of his work. De Witt's maxim was like Cecil's: "One thing at a time." "If," said he, "I have any necessary despatches to make, I think of nothing else till they are finished; if any domestic affairs require my attention, I give myself wholly up to them till they are set in order."

A French minister, who was alike remarkable for his despatch of business and his constant attendance at places of amusement, being asked how he contrived to combine both objects, replied, "Simply by never postponing till to-morrow what should be done to-day." Lord Brougham has said that a certain English statesman reversed the process, and that his maxim was, never to transact to-day what could be postponed till to-morrow. Unhappily, such is the practice of many besides that minister, already almost forgotten; the practice is that of the indolent and the unsuccessful. Such men, too, are apt to rely upon agents, who are not always to be relied upon. Important affairs must be attended to in person. "If you want your business done," says the proverb, "go and do it; if you don't want it done, send some one else."

An indolent country gentleman had a freehold estate producing about five hundred a-year. Becoming involved in debt, he sold half the estate, and let the remainder to an industrious farmer for twenty years. About the end of the term the farmer called to pay his rent, and asked the owner whether he would sell the farm. "Will you buy it?" asked the owner, surprised. "Yes, if we can agree about the price." "That is exceedingly strange," observed the gentleman; "pray, tell me how it happens that, while I could not live upon twice as much land for which I paid no rent, you are regularly paying me two hundred a-year for your farm, and are able, in a few years, to purchase it." "The reason is plain," was the reply; "you sat still and said Go, I got up and said Come; you laid in bed and enjoyed your estate, I rose in the morning and minded my business."

Sir Walter Scott, writing to a youth who had obtained a situation and asked for his advice, gave him in reply this sound counsel: "Beware of stumbling over a propensity which easily besets you from not having your time fully employed—I mean what the women call dawdling. Your motto must be, Hoc age. Do instantly whatever is to be done, and take the hours of recreation after business, never before it. When a regiment is under march, the rear is often thrown into confusion because the front do not move steadily and without interruption. It is the same with business. If that which is first in hand is not instantly, steadily, and regularly despatched, other things accumulate behind, till affairs begin to press all at once, and no human brain can stand the confusion."

Promptitude in action may be stimulated by a due consideration of the value of time. An Italian philosopher was accustomed to call time his estate: an estate which produces nothing of value without cultivation, but, duly improved, never fails to recompense the labours of the diligent worker. Allowed to lie waste, the product will be only noxious weeds and vicious growths of all kinds. One of the minor uses of steady employment is, that it keeps one out of mischief, for truly an idle brain is the devil's workshop, and a lazy man the devil's bolster. To be occupied is to be possessed as by a tenant, whereas to be idle is to be empty; and when the doors of the imagination are opened, temptation finds a ready access, and evil thoughts come trooping in. It is observed at sea, that men are never so much disposed to grumble and mutiny as when least employed. Hence an old captain, when there was nothing else to do, would issue the order to "scour the anchor!"

Men of business are accustomed to quote the maxim that Time is money; but it is more; the proper improvement of it is self-culture, self-improvement, and growth of character. An hour wasted daily on trifles or in indolence, would, if devoted to self-improvement, make an ignorant man wise in a few years, and employed in good works, would make his life fruitful, and death a harvest of worthy deeds. Fifteen minutes a day devoted to self-improvement, will be felt at the end of the year. Good thoughts and carefully gathered experience take up no room, and may be carried about as our companions everywhere, without cost or incumbrance. An economical use of time is the true mode of securing leisure: it enables us to get through business and carry it forward, instead of being driven by it. On the other hand, the miscalculation of time involves us in perpetual hurry, confusion, and difficulties; and life becomes a mere shuffle of expedients, usually followed by disaster. Nelson once said, "I owe all my success in life to having been always a quarter of an hour before my time."

Some take no thought of the value of money until they have come to an end of it, and many do the same with their time. The hours are allowed to flow by unemployed, and then, when life is fast waning, they bethink themselves of the duty of making a wiser use of it. But the habit of listlessness and idleness may already have become confirmed, and they are unable to break the bonds with which they have permitted themselves to become bound.

Lost wealth may be replaced by industry, lost knowledge by study, lost health by temperance or medicine, but lost time is gone for ever.

A proper consideration of the value of time, will also inspire habits of punctuality. "Punctuality," said Louis XIV., "is the politeness of kings." It is also the duty of gentlemen, and the necessity of men of business. Nothing begets confidence in a man sooner than the practice of this virtue, and nothing shakes confidence sooner than the want of it. He who holds to his appointment and does not keep you waiting for him, shows that he has regard for your time as well as for his own. Thus punctuality is one of the modes by which we testify our personal respect for those whom we are called upon to meet in the business of life. It is also conscientiousness in a measure; for an appointment is a contract, express or implied, and he who does not keep it breaks faith, as well as dishonestly uses other people's time, and thus inevitably loses character. We naturally come to the conclusion that the person who is careless about time will be careless about business, and that he is not the one to be trusted with the transaction of matters of importance. When Washington's secretary excused himself for the lateness of his attendance and laid the blame upon his watch, his master quietly said, "Then you must get another watch, or I another secretary."

The person who is negligent of time and its employment is usually found to be a general disturber of others' peace and serenity. It was wittily said by Lord Chesterfield of the old Duke of Newcastle—"His Grace loses an hour in the morning, and is looking for it all the rest of the day." Everybody with whom the unpunctual man has to do is thrown from time to time into a state of fever: he is systematically late; regular only in his irregularity. He conducts his dawdling as if upon system; arrives at his appointment after time; gets to the railway station after the train has started; posts his letter when the box has closed. Thus business is thrown into confusion, and everybody concerned is put out of temper. It will generally be found that the men who are thus habitually behind time are as habitually behind success; and the world generally casts them aside to swell the ranks of the grumblers and the railers against fortune.

In addition to the ordinary working qualities the business man of the highest class requires quick perception and firmness in the execution of his plans. Tact is also important; and though this is partly the gift of nature, it is yet capable of being cultivated and developed by observation and experience. Men of this quality are quick to see the right mode of action, and if they have decision of purpose, are prompt to carry out their undertakings to a successful issue. These qualities are especially valuable, and indeed indispensable, in those who direct the action of other men on a large scale, as for instance, in the case of the commander of an army in the field. It is not merely necessary that the general should be great as a warrior but also as a man of business. He must possess great tact, much knowledge of character, and ability to organize the movements of a large mass of men, whom he has to feed, clothe, and furnish with whatever may be necessary in order that they may keep the field and win battles. In these respects Napoleon and Wellington were both first-rate men of business.

Though Napoleon had an immense love for details, he had also a vivid power of imagination, which enabled him to look along extended lines of action, and deal with those details on a large scale, with judgment and rapidity. He possessed such knowledge of character as enabled him to select, almost unerringly, the best agents for the execution of his designs. But he trusted as little as possible to agents in matters of great moment, on which important results depended. This feature in his character is illustrated in a remarkable degree by the 'Napoleon Correspondence,' now in course of publication, and particularly by the contents of the 15th volume, [277] which include the letters, orders, and despatches, written by the Emperor at Finkenstein, a little chateau on the frontier of Poland in the year 1807, shortly after the victory of Eylau.

The French army was then lying encamped along the river Passarge with the Russians before them, the Austrians on their right flank, and the conquered Prussians in their rear. A long line of communications had to be maintained with France, through a hostile country; but so carefully, and with such foresight was this provided for, that it is said Napoleon never missed a post. The movements of armies, the bringing up of reinforcements from remote points in France, Spain, Italy, and Germany, the opening of canals and the levelling of roads to enable the produce of Poland and Prussia to be readily transported to his encampments, had his unceasing attention, down to the minutest details. We find him directing where horses were to be obtained, making arrangements for an adequate supply of saddles, ordering shoes for the soldiers, and specifying the number of rations of bread, biscuit, and spirits, that were to be brought to camp, or stored in magazines for the use of the troops. At the same time we find him writing to Paris giving directions for the reorganization of the French College, devising a scheme of public education, dictating bulletins and articles for the 'Moniteur,' revising the details of the budgets, giving instructions to architects as to alterations to be made at the Tuileries and the Church of the Madelaine, throwing an occasional sarcasm at Madame de Stael and the Parisian journals, interfering to put down a squabble at the Grand Opera, carrying on a correspondence with the Sultan of Turkey and the Schah of Persia, so that while his body was at Finkenstein, his mind seemed to be working at a hundred different places in Paris, in Europe, and throughout the world.

We find him in one letter asking Ney if he has duly received the muskets which have been sent him; in another he gives directions to Prince Jerome as to the shirts, greatcoats, clothes, shoes, shakos, and arms, to be served out to the Wurtemburg regiments; again he presses Cambacérès to forward to the army a double stock of corn—"The ifs and the buts," said he, "are at present out of season, and above all it must be done with speed." Then he informs Daru that the army want shirts, and that they don't come to hand. To Massena he writes, "Let me know if your biscuit and bread arrangements are yet completed." To the Grand due de Berg, he gives directions as to the accoutrements of the cuirassiers— "They complain that the men want sabres; send an officer to obtain them at Posen. It is also said they want helmets; order that they be made at Ebling. . . . It is not by sleeping that one can accomplish anything." Thus no point of detail was neglected, and the energies of all were stimulated into action with extraordinary power. Though many of the Emperor's days were occupied by inspections of his troops,—in the course of which he sometimes rode from thirty to forty leagues a day,—and by reviews, receptions, and affairs of state, leaving but little time for business matters, he neglected nothing on that account; but devoted the greater part of his nights, when necessary, to examining budgets, dictating dispatches, and attending to the thousand matters of detail in the organization and working of the Imperial Government; the machinery of which was for the most part concentrated in his own head.

Like Napoleon, the Duke of Wellington was a first-rate man of business; and it is not perhaps saying too much to aver that it was in no small degree because of his possession of a business faculty amounting to genius, that the Duke never lost a battle.

While a subaltern, he became dissatisfied with the slowness of his promotion, and having passed from the infantry to the cavalry twice, and back again, without advancement, he applied to Lord Camden, then Viceroy of Ireland, for employment in the Revenue or Treasury Board. Had he succeeded, no doubt he would have made a first-rate head of a department, as he would have made a first-rate merchant or manufacturer. But his application failed, and he remained with the army to become the greatest of British generals.

The Duke began his active military career under the Duke of York and General Walmoden, in Flanders and Holland, where he learnt, amidst misfortunes and defeats, how bad business arrangements and bad generalship serve to ruin the morale of an army. Ten years after entering the army we find him a colonel in India, reported by his superiors as an officer of indefatigable energy and application. He entered into the minutest details of the service, and sought to raise the discipline of his men to the highest standard. "The regiment of Colonel Wellesley," wrote General Harris in 1799, "is a model regiment; on the score of soldierly bearing, discipline, instruction, and orderly behaviour it is above all praise." Thus qualifying himself for posts of greater confidence, he was shortly after nominated governor of the capital of Mysore. In the war with the Mahrattas he was first called upon to try his hand at generalship; and at thirty-four he won the memorable battle of Assaye, with an army composed of 1500 British and 5000 sepoys, over 20,000 Mahratta infantry and 30,000 cavalry. But so brilliant a victory did not in the least disturb his equanimity, or affect the perfect honesty of his character.

Shortly after this event the opportunity occurred for exhibiting his admirable practical qualities as an administrator. Placed in command of an important district immediately after the capture of Seringapatam, his first object was to establish rigid order and discipline among his own men. Flushed with victory, the troops were found riotous and disorderly. "Send me the provost marshal," said he, "and put him under my orders: till some of the marauders are hung, it is impossible to expect order or safety." This rigid severity of Wellington in the field, though it was the dread, proved the salvation of his troops in many campaigns. His next step was to re-establish the markets and re-open the sources of supply. General Harris wrote to the Governor-general, strongly commending Colonel Wellesley for the perfect discipline he had established, and for his "judicious and masterly arrangements in respect to supplies, which opened an abundant free market, and inspired confidence into dealers of every description." The same close attention to, and mastery of details, characterized him throughout his Indian career; and it is remarkable that one of his ablest despatches to Lord Clive, full of practical information as to the conduct of the campaign, was written whilst the column he commanded was crossing the Toombuddra, in the face of the vastly superior army of Dhoondiah, posted on the opposite bank, and while a thousand matters of the deepest interest were pressing upon the commander's mind. But it was one of his most remarkable characteristics, thus to be able to withdraw himself temporarily from the business immediately in hand, and to bend his full powers upon the consideration of matters totally distinct; even the most difficult circumstances on such occasions failing to embarrass or intimidate him.

Returned to England with a reputation for generalship, Sir Arthur Wellesley met with immediate employment. In 1808 a corps of 10,000 men destined to liberate Portugal was placed under his charge. He landed, fought, and won two battles, and signed the Convention of Cintra. After the death of Sir John Moore he was entrusted with the command of a new expedition to Portugal. But Wellington was fearfully overmatched throughout his Peninsular campaigns. From 1809 to 1813 he never had more than 30,000 British troops under his command, at a time when there stood opposed to him in the Peninsula some 350,000 French, mostly veterans, led by some of Napoleon's ablest generals. How was he to contend against such immense forces with any fair prospect of success? His clear discernment and strong common sense soon taught him that he must adopt a different policy from that of the Spanish generals, who were invariably beaten and dispersed whenever they ventured to offer battle in the open plains. He perceived he had yet to create the army that was to contend against the French with any reasonable chance of success. Accordingly, after the battle of Talavera in 1809, when he found himself encompassed on all sides by superior forces of French, he retired into Portugal, there to carry out the settled policy on which he had by this time determined. It was, to organise a Portuguese army under British officers, and teach them to act in combination with his own troops, in the mean time avoiding the peril of a defeat by declining all engagements. He would thus, he conceived, destroy the morale of the French, who could not exist without victories; and when his army was ripe for action, and the enemy demoralized, he would then fall upon them with all his might.

The extraordinary qualities displayed by Lord Wellington throughout these immortal campaigns, can only be appreciated after a perusal of his despatches, which contain the unvarnished tale of the manifold ways and means by which he laid the foundations of his success. Never was man more tried by difficulty and opposition, arising not less from the imbecility, falsehoods and intrigues of the British Government of the day, than from the selfishness, cowardice, and vanity of the people he went to save. It may, indeed, be said of him, that he sustained the war in Spain by his individual firmness and self-reliance, which never failed him even in the midst of his great discouragements. He had not only to fight Napoleon's veterans, but also to hold in check the Spanish juntas and the Portuguese regency. He had the utmost difficulty in obtaining provisions and clothing for his troops; and it will scarcely be credited that, while engaged with the enemy in the battle of Talavera, the Spaniards, who ran away, fell upon the baggage of the British army, and the ruffians actually plundered it! These and other vexations the Duke bore with a sublime patience and self-control, and held on his course, in the face of ingratitude, treachery, and opposition, with indomitable firmness. He neglected nothing, and attended to every important detail of business himself. When he found that food for his troops was not to be obtained from England, and that he must rely upon his own resources for feeding them, he forthwith commenced business as a corn merchant on a large scale, in copartnery with the British Minister at Lisbon. Commissariat bills were created, with which grain was bought in the ports of the Mediterranean and in South America. When he had thus filled his magazines, the overplus was sold to the Portuguese, who were greatly in want of provisions. He left nothing whatever to chance, but provided for every contingency. He gave his attention to the minutest details of the service; and was accustomed to concentrate his whole energies, from time to time, on such apparently ignominious matters as soldiers' shoes, camp-kettles, biscuits and horse fodder. His magnificent business qualities were everywhere felt, and there can be no doubt that, by the care with which he provided for every contingency, and the personal attention which he gave to every detail, he laid the foundations of his great success. [283] By such means he transformed an army of raw levies into the best soldiers in Europe, with whom he declared it to be possible to go anywhere and do anything.

We have already referred to his remarkable power of abstracting himself from the work, no matter how engrossing, immediately in hand, and concentrating his energies upon the details of some entirely different business. Thus Napier relates that it was while he was preparing to fight the battle of Salamanca that he had to expose to the Ministers at home the futility of relying upon a loan; it was on the heights of San Christoval, on the field of battle itself, that he demonstrated the absurdity of attempting to establish a Portuguese bank; it was in the trenches of Burgos that he dissected Funchal's scheme of

156

finance, and exposed the folly of attempting the sale of church property; and on each occasion, he showed himself as well acquainted with these subjects as with the minutest detail in the mechanism of armies.

Another feature in his character, showing the upright man of business, was his thorough honesty. Whilst Soult ransacked and carried away with him from Spain numerous pictures of great value, Wellington did not appropriate to himself a single farthing's worth of property. Everywhere he paid his way, even when in the enemy's country. When he had crossed the French frontier, followed by 40,000 Spaniards, who sought to "make fortunes" by pillage and plunder, he first rebuked their officers, and then, finding his efforts to restrain them unavailing, he sent them back into their own country. It is a remarkable fact, that, even in France the peasantry fled from their own countrymen, and carried their valuables within the protection of the British lines! At the very same time, Wellington was writing home to the British Ministry, "We are overwhelmed with debts, and I can scarcely stir out of my house on account of public creditors waiting to demand payment of what is due to them." Jules Maurel, in his estimate of the Duke's character, says, "Nothing can be grander or more nobly original than this admission. This old soldier, after thirty years' service, this iron man and victorious general, established in an enemy's country at the head of an immense army, is afraid of his creditors! This is a kind of fear that has seldom troubled the mind of conquerors and invaders; and I doubt if the annals of war could present anything comparable to this sublime simplicity." But the Duke himself, had the matter been put to him, would most probably have disclaimed any intention of acting even grandly or nobly in the matter; merely regarding the punctual payment of his debts as the best and most honourable mode of conducting his business.

The truth of the good old maxim, that "Honesty is the

best policy," is upheld by the daily experience of life; uprightness and integrity being found as successful in business as in everything else. As Hugh Miller's worthy uncle used to advise him, "In all your dealings give your neighbour the cast of the bank—'good measure, heaped up, and running over,'—and you will not lose by it in the end." A well-known brewer of beer attributed his success to the liberality with which he used his malt. Going up to the vat and tasting it, he would say, "Still rather poor, my lads; give it another cast of the malt." The brewer put his character into his beer, and it proved generous accordingly, obtaining a reputation in England, India, and the colonies, which laid the foundation of a large fortune. Integrity of word and deed ought to be the very cornerstone of all business transactions. To the tradesman, the merchant, and manufacturer, it should be what honour is to the soldier, and charity to the Christian. In the humblest calling there will always be found scope for the exercise of this uprightness of character. Hugh Miller speaks of the mason with whom he served his apprenticeship, as one who "put his conscience into every stone that he laid." So the true mechanic will pride himself upon the thoroughness and solidity of his work, and the high-minded contractor upon the honesty of performance of his contract in every particular. The upright manufacturer will find not only honour and reputation, but substantial success, in the genuineness of the article which he produces, and the merchant in the honesty of what he sells, and that it really is what it seems to be. Baron Dupin, speaking of the general probity of Englishmen, which he held to be a principal cause of their success, observed, "We may succeed for a time by fraud, by surprise, by violence; but we can succeed permanently only by means directly opposite. It is not alone the courage, the intelligence, the activity, of the merchant and manufacturer which maintain the superiority of their productions and the character of their country; it is far more their wisdom, their economy, and, above all, their probity. If ever in the British Islands the useful citizen should lose these virtues, we may be sure that, for England, as for every other country, the vessels of a degenerate commerce, repulsed from every shore, would speedily disappear from those seas whose surface they now cover with the treasures of the universe, bartered for the treasures of the industry of the three kingdoms."

It must be admitted, that Trade tries character perhaps more severely than any other pursuit in life. It puts to the severest tests honesty, self-denial, justice, and truthfulness; and men of business who pass through such trials unstained are perhaps worthy of as great honour as soldiers who prove their courage amidst the fire and perils of battle. And, to the credit of the multitudes of men engaged in the various departments of trade, we think it must be admitted that on the whole they pass through their trials nobly. If we reflect but for a moment on the vast amount of wealth daily entrusted even to subordinate persons, who themselves probably earn but a bare competency—the loose cash which is constantly passing through the hands of shopmen, agents, brokers, and clerks in banking houses,—and note how comparatively few are the breaches of trust which occur amidst all this temptation, it will probably be admitted that this steady daily honesty of conduct is most honourable to human nature, if it do not even tempt us to be proud of it. The same trust and confidence reposed by men of business in each other, as implied by the system of Credit, which is mainly based upon the principle of honour, would be surprising if it were not so much a matter of ordinary practice in business transactions. Dr. Chalmers has well said, that the implicit trust with which merchants are accustomed to confide in distant agents, separated from them perhaps by half the globe—often consigning vast wealth to persons, recommended only by their character, whom perhaps they have never seen—is probably the finest act of homage which men can render to one another.

Although common honesty is still happily in the ascendant amongst common people, and the general business community of England is still sound at heart, putting their honest character into their respective callings,—there are unhappily, as there have been in all times, but too many instances of flagrant dishonesty and fraud, exhibited by the unscrupulous, the over-speculative, and the intensely selfish in their haste to be rich. There are tradesmen who adulterate, contractors who "scamp," manufacturers who give us shoddy instead of wool, "dressing" instead of cotton, cast-iron tools instead of steel, needles without eyes, razors made only "to sell," and swindled fabrics in many shapes. But these we must hold to be the exceptional cases, of low-minded and grasping men, who, though they may gain wealth which they probably cannot enjoy, will never gain an honest character, nor secure that without which wealth is nothing—a heart at peace. "The rogue cozened not me, but his own conscience," said Bishop Latimer of a cutler who made him pay twopence for a knife not worth a penny. Money, earned by screwing, cheating, and overreaching, may for a time dazzle the eyes of the unthinking; but the bubbles blown by unscrupulous rogues, when full-blown, usually glitter only to burst. The Sadleirs, Dean Pauls, and Redpaths, for the most part, come to a sad end even in this world; and though the successful swindles of others may not be "found out," and the gains of their roguery may remain with them, it will be as a curse and not as a blessing.

It is possible that the scrupulously honest man may not grow rich so fast as the unscrupulous and dishonest one; but the success will be of a truer kind, earned without fraud or injustice. And even though a man should for a time be unsuccessful, still he must be honest: better lose all and save character. For character is itself a fortune; and if the high-principled man will but hold on his way courageously, success will surely come,—nor will the highest reward of all be withheld from him. Wordsworth well describes the "Happy Warrior," as he

"Who comprehends his trust, and to the same
Keeps faithful with a singleness of aim;
And therefore does not stoop, nor lie in wait
For wealth, or honour, or for worldly state;
Whom they must follow, on whose head must fall,
Like showers of manna, if they come at all."

As an example of the high-minded mercantile man trained in upright habits of business, and distinguished for justice, truthfulness, and honesty of dealing in all things, the career of the well-known David Barclay, grandson of Robert Barclay, of Ury, the author of the celebrated 'Apology for the Quakers,' may be briefly referred to. For many years he was the head of an extensive house in Cheapside, chiefly engaged in the American trade; but like Granville Sharp, he entertained so strong an opinion against the war with our American colonies, that he determined to retire altogether from the trade. Whilst a merchant, he was as much distinguished for his talents, knowledge, integrity, and power, as he afterwards was for his patriotism and munificent philanthropy. He was a mirror of truthfulness and honesty; and, as became the good Christian and true gentleman, his word was always held to be as good as his bond. His position, and his high character, induced the Ministers of the day on many occasions to seek his advice; and, when examined before the House of Commons on the subject of the American dispute, his views were so clearly expressed, and his advice was so strongly justified by the reasons stated by him, that Lord North publicly acknowledged that he had derived more information from David Barclay than from all others east of Temple Bar. On retiring from business, it was not to rest in luxurious ease, but to enter upon new labours of usefulness for others. With ample means, he felt that he still owed to society the duty of a good example. He founded a house of industry near his residence at Walthamstow, which he supported at a heavy outlay for several years, until at length he succeeded in rendering it a source of comfort as well as independence to the well-disposed families of the poor in that neighbourhood. When an estate in Jamaica fell to him, he determined, though at a cost of some 10,000l., at once to give liberty to the whole of the slaves on the property. He sent out an agent, who hired a ship, and he had the little slave community transported to one of the free American states, where they settled down and prospered. Mr. Barclay had been assured that the negroes were too ignorant and too barbarous for freedom, and it was thus that he determined practically to demonstrate the fallacy of the assertion. In dealing with his accumulated savings, he made himself the executor of his own will, and instead of leaving a large fortune to be divided among his relatives at his death, he extended to them his munificent aid during his life, watched and aided them in their respective careers, and thus not only laid the foundation, but lived to see the maturity, of some of the largest and most prosperous business concerns in the metropolis. We believe that to this day some of our most eminent merchants—such as the Gurneys, Hanburys, and Buxtons—are proud to acknowledge with gratitude the obligations they owe to David Barclay for the means of their first introduction to life, and for the benefits of his counsel and countenance in the early stages of their career. Such a man stands as a mark of the mercantile honesty and integrity of his country, and is a model and example for men of business in all time to come.

APPLICATION AND PERSEVERANCE.

"Rich are the diligent, who can command
Time, nature's stock! and could his hour-glass fall,
Would, as for seed of stars, stoop for the sand,
And, by incessant labour, gather all."—D'Avenant.

"Allez en avant, et la foi vous viendra!"—D'Alembert.

THE greatest results in life are usually attained by simple means, and the exercise of ordinary qualities. The common life of every day, with its cares, necessities, and duties, affords ample opportunity for acquiring experience of the best kind; and its most beaten paths provide the true worker with abundant scope for effort and room for self-improvement. The road of human welfare lies along the old highway of steadfast well-doing; and they who are the most persistent, and work in the truest spirit, will usually be the most successful.

Fortune has often been blamed for her blindness; but fortune is not so blind as men are. Those who look into practical life will find that fortune is usually on the side of the industrious, as the winds and waves are on the side of the best navigators. In the pursuit of even the highest branches of human inquiry, the commoner qualities are found the most useful—such as common sense, attention, application, and perseverance. Genius may not be necessary, though even genius of the highest sort does not disdain the use of these ordinary qualities. The very greatest men have been among the least believers in the power of genius, and as worldly wise and persevering as successful men of the commoner sort. Some have even defined genius to be only common sense intensified. A distinguished teacher and president of a college spoke of it as the power of making efforts. John Foster held it to be the power of lighting one's own fire. Buffon said of genius "it is patience."

Newton's was unquestionably a mind of the very highest order, and yet, when asked by what means he had worked out his extraordinary discoveries, he modestly answered, "By always thinking unto them." At another time he thus expressed his method of study: "I keep the subject continually before me, and wait till the first dawnings open slowly by little and little into a full and clear light." It was in Newton's case, as in every other, only by diligent application and perseverance that his great reputation was achieved. Even his recreation consisted in change of study, laying down one subject to take up another. To Dr. Bentley he said: "If I have done the public any service, it is due to nothing but industry and patient thought." So Kepler, another great philosopher, speaking of his studies and his progress, said: "As in Virgil, 'Fama mobilitate viget, vires acquirit eundo,' so it was with me, that the diligent thought on these things was the occasion of still further thinking; until at last I brooded with the whole energy of my mind upon the subject."

The extraordinary results effected by dint of sheer industry and perseverance, have led many distinguished men to doubt whether the gift of genius be so exceptional an endowment as it is usually supposed to be. Thus Voltaire held that it is only a very slight line of separation that divides the man of genius from the man of ordinary mould. Beccaria was even of opinion that all men might be poets and orators, and Reynolds that they might be painters and sculptors. If this were really so, that stolid Englishman might not have been so very far wrong after all, who, on Canova's death, inquired of his brother whether it was "his intention to carry on the business!" Locke, Helvetius, and Diderot believed that all men have an equal aptitude for genius, and that what some are able to effect, under the laws which regulate the operations of the intellect, must also be within the reach of others who, under like circumstances, apply themselves to like pursuits. But while admitting to the fullest extent the wonderful achievements of labour, and recognising the fact that men of the most distinguished genius have invariably been found the most indefatigable workers, it must nevertheless be sufficiently obvious that, without the original endowment of heart and brain, no amount of labour, however well applied, could have produced a Shakespeare, a Newton, a Beethoven, or a Michael Angelo.

Dalton, the chemist, repudiated the notion of his being

"a genius," attributing everything which he had accomplished to simple industry and accumulation. John Hunter said of himself, "My mind is like a beehive; but full as it is of buzz and apparent confusion, it is yet full of order and regularity, and food collected with incessant industry from the choicest stores of nature." We have, indeed, but to glance at the biographies of great men to find that the most distinguished inventors, artists, thinkers, and workers of all kinds, owe their success, in a great measure, to their indefatigable industry and application. They were men who turned all things to gold—even time itself. Disraeli the elder held that the secret of success consisted in being master of your subject, such mastery being attainable only through continuous application and study. Hence it happens that the men who have most moved the world, have not been so much men of genius, strictly so called, as men of intense mediocre abilities, and untiring perseverance; not so often the gifted, of naturally bright and shining qualities, as those who have applied themselves diligently to their work, in whatsoever line that might lie. "Alas!" said a widow, speaking of her brilliant but careless son, "he has not the gift of continuance." Wanting in perseverance, such volatile natures are outstripped in the race of life by the diligent and even the dull. "Che va piano, va longano, e va lontano," says the Italian proverb: Who goes slowly, goes long, and goes far.

Hence, a great point to be aimed at is to get the working quality well trained. When that is done, the race will be found comparatively easy. We must repeat and again repeat; facility will come with labour. Not even the simplest art can be accomplished without it; and what difficulties it is found capable of achieving! It was by early discipline and repetition that the late Sir Robert Peel cultivated those remarkable, though still mediocre powers, which rendered him so illustrious an ornament of the British Senate. When a boy at Drayton Manor, his father was accustomed to set him up at table to practise speaking extempore; and he early accustomed him to repeat as much of the Sunday's sermon as he could remember. Little progress was made at first, but by steady perseverance the habit of attention became powerful, and the sermon was at length repeated almost verbatim. When afterwards replying in succession to the arguments of his parliamentary opponents—an art in which he was perhaps unrivalled—it was little surmised that the extraordinary power of accurate remembrance which he displayed on such occasions had been originally trained under the discipline of his father in the parish church of Drayton.

It is indeed marvellous what continuous application will effect in the commonest of things. It may seem a simple affair to play upon a violin; yet what a long and laborious practice it requires! Giardini said to a youth who asked him how long it would take to learn it, "Twelve hours a day for twenty years together." Industry, it is said, fait l'ours danser. The poor figurante must devote years of incessant toil to her profitless task before she can shine in it. When Taglioni was preparing herself for her evening exhibition, she would, after a severe two hours' lesson from her father, fall down exhausted, and had to be undressed, sponged, and resuscitated totally unconscious. The agility and bounds of the evening were insured only at a price like this.

Progress, however, of the best kind, is comparatively slow. Great results cannot be achieved at once; and we must be satisfied to advance in life as we walk, step by step. De Maistre says that "to know how to wait is the great secret of success." We must sow before we can reap, and often have to wait long, content meanwhile to look patiently forward in hope; the fruit best worth waiting for often ripening the slowest. But "time and patience," says the Eastern proverb, "change the mulberry leaf to satin."

To wait patiently, however, men must work cheerfully. Cheerfulness is an excellent working quality, imparting great elasticity to the character. As a bishop has said,

"Temper is nine-tenths of Christianity;" so are cheerfulness and diligence nine-tenths of practical wisdom. They are the life and soul of success, as well as of happiness; perhaps the very highest pleasure in life consisting in clear, brisk, conscious working; energy, confidence, and every other good quality mainly depending upon it. Sydney Smith, when labouring as a parish priest at Foston-le-Clay, in Yorkshire,—though he did not feel himself to be in his proper element,—went cheerfully to work in the firm determination to do his best. "I am resolved," he said, "to like it, and reconcile myself to it, which is more manly than to feign myself above it, and to send up complaints by the post of being thrown away, and being desolate, and such like trash." So Dr. Hook, when leaving Leeds for a new sphere of labour said, "Wherever I may be, I shall, by God's blessing, do with my might what my hand findeth to do; and if I do not find work, I shall make it."

Labourers for the public good especially, have to work long and patiently, often uncheered by the prospect of immediate recompense or result. The seeds they sow sometimes lie hidden under the winter's snow, and before the spring comes the husbandman may have gone to his rest. It is not every public worker who, like Rowland Hill, sees his great idea bring forth fruit in his life-time. Adam Smith sowed the seeds of a great social amelioration in that dingy old University of Glasgow where he so long laboured, and laid the foundations of his 'Wealth of Nations;' but seventy years passed before his work bore substantial fruits, nor indeed are they all gathered in yet.

Nothing can compensate for the loss of hope in a man: it entirely changes the character. "How can I work—how can I be happy," said a great but miserable thinker, "when I have lost all hope?" One of the most cheerful and courageous, because one of the most hopeful of workers, was Carey, the missionary. When in India, it was no uncommon thing for him to weary out three pundits, who officiated as his clerks, in one day, he himself taking rest only in change of employment. Carey, the son of a shoe-maker, was supported in his labours by Ward, the son of a carpenter, and Marsham, the son of a weaver. By their labours, a magnificent college was erected at Serampore; sixteen flourishing stations were established; the Bible was translated into sixteen languages, and the seeds were sown of a beneficent moral revolution in British India. Carey was never ashamed of the humbleness of his origin. On one occasion, when at the Governor-General's table he over-heard an officer opposite him asking another, loud enough to be heard, whether Carey had not once been a shoemaker: "No, sir," exclaimed Carey immediately; "only a cobbler." An eminently characteristic anecdote has been told of his perseverance as a boy. When climbing a tree one day, his foot slipped, and he fell to the ground, breaking his leg by the fall. He was confined to his bed for weeks, but when he recovered and was able to walk without support, the very first thing he did was to go and climb that tree. Carey had need of this sort of dauntless courage for the great missionary work of his life, and nobly and resolutely he did it.

It was a maxim of Dr. Young, the philosopher, that "Any man can do what any other man has done;" and it is unquestionable that he himself never recoiled from any trials to which he determined to subject himself. It is related of him, that the first time he mounted a horse, he was in company with the grandson of Mr. Barclay of Ury, the well-known sportsman; when the horseman who preceded them leapt a high fence. Young wished to imitate him, but fell off his horse in the attempt. Without saying a word, he remounted, made a second effort, and was again unsuccessful, but this time he was not thrown further than on to the horse's neck, to which he clung. At the third trial, he succeeded, and cleared the fence.

The story of Timour the Tartar learning a lesson of perseverance under adversity from the spider is well known. Not less interesting is the anecdote of Audubon, the American ornithologist, as related by himself: "An accident," he says, "which happened to two hundred of my original drawings, nearly put a stop to my researches in ornithology. I shall relate it, merely to show how far enthusiasm—for by no other name can I call my perseverance—may enable the preserver of nature to surmount the most disheartening difficulties. I left the village of Henderson, in Kentucky, situated on the banks of the Ohio, where I resided for several years, to proceed to Philadelphia on business. I looked to my drawings before my departure, placed them carefully in a wooden box, and gave them in charge of a relative, with injunctions to see that no injury should happen to them. My absence was of several months; and when I returned, after having enjoyed the pleasures of home for a few days, I inquired after my box, and what I was pleased to call my treasure. The box was produced and opened; but reader, feel for me—a pair of Norway rats had taken possession of the whole, and reared a young family among the gnawed bits of paper, which, but a month previous, represented nearly a thousand inhabitants of air! The burning beat which instantly rushed through my brain was too great to be endured without affecting my whole nervous system. I slept for several nights, and the days passed like days of oblivion—until the animal powers being recalled into action through the strength of my constitution, I took up my gun, my notebook, and my pencils, and went forth to the woods as gaily as if nothing had happened. I felt pleased that I might now make better drawings than before; and, ere a period not exceeding three years had elapsed, my portfolio was again filled."

The accidental destruction of Sir Isaac Newton's papers, by his little dog 'Diamond' upsetting a lighted taper upon his desk, by which the elaborate calculations of many years were in a moment destroyed, is a well-known anecdote, and need not be repeated: it is said that the loss caused the philosopher such profound grief that it seriously injured his health, and impaired his understanding. An accident of a somewhat similar kind happened to the MS. of Mr. Carlyle's first volume of his 'French Revolution.' He had lent the MS. to a literary neighbour to peruse. By some mischance, it had been left lying on the parlour floor, and become forgotten. Weeks ran on, and the historian sent for his work, the printers being loud for "copy." Inquiries were made, and it was found that the maid-of-all-work, finding what she conceived to be a bundle of waste paper on the floor, had used it to light the kitchen and parlour fires with! Such was the answer returned to Mr. Carlyle; and his feelings may be imagined. There was, however, no help for him but to set resolutely to work to re-write the book; and he turned to and did it. He had no draft, and was compelled to rake up from his memory facts, ideas, and expressions, which had been long since dismissed. The composition of the book in the first instance had been a work of pleasure; the re-writing of it a second time was one of pain and anguish almost beyond belief. That he persevered and finished the volume under such circumstances, affords an instance of determination of purpose which has seldom been surpassed.

The lives of eminent inventors are eminently illustrative of the same quality of perseverance. George Stephenson, when addressing young men, was accustomed to sum up his best advice to them, in the words, "Do as I have done—persevere." He had worked at the improvement of his locomotive for some fifteen years before achieving his decisive victory at Rainhill; and Watt was engaged for some thirty years upon the condensing-engine before he brought it to perfection. But there are equally striking illustrations of perseverance to be found in every other branch of science, art, and industry. Perhaps one of the most interesting is that connected with the disentombment of the Nineveh marbles, and the discovery of the long-lost cuneiform or arrow-headed character in which the inscriptions on them are written—a kind of writing which had been lost to the world since the period of the Macedonian conquest of Persia.

An intelligent cadet of the East India Company, stationed at Kermanshah, in Persia, had observed the curious cuneiform inscriptions on the old monuments in the neighbourhood—so old that all historical traces of them had been lost,—and amongst the inscriptions which he copied was that on the celebrated rock of Behistun—a perpendicular rock rising abruptly some 1700 feet from the plain, the lower part bearing inscriptions for the space of about 300 feet in three languages—Persian, Scythian, and Assyrian. Comparison of the known with the unknown, of the language which survived with the language that had been lost, enabled this cadet to acquire some knowledge of the cuneiform character, and even to form an alphabet. Mr. (afterwards Sir Henry) Rawlinson sent his tracings home for examination. No professors in colleges as yet knew anything of the cuneiform character; but there was a ci-devant clerk of the East India House—a modest unknown man of the name of Norris—who had made this little-understood subject his study, to whom the tracings were submitted; and so accurate was his knowledge, that, though he had never seen the Behistun rock, he pronounced that the cadet had not copied the puzzling inscription with proper exactness. Rawlinson, who was still in the neighbourhood of the rock, compared his copy with the original, and found that Norris was right; and by further comparison and careful study the knowledge of the cuneiform writing was thus greatly advanced.

But to make the learning of these two self-taught men of avail, a third labourer was necessary in order to supply them with material for the exercise of their skill. Such a labourer presented himself in the person of Austen Layard, originally an articled clerk in the office of a London solicitor. One would scarcely have expected to find in these three men, a cadet, an India-House clerk, and a lawyer's clerk, the discoverers of a forgotten language, and of the buried history of Babylon; yet it was so. Layard was a youth of only twenty-two, travelling in the East, when he was possessed with a desire to penetrate the regions beyond the Euphrates. Accompanied by a single companion, trusting to his arms for protection, and, what was better, to his cheerfulness, politeness, and chivalrous bearing, he passed safely amidst tribes at deadly war with each other; and, after the lapse of many years, with comparatively slender means at his command, but aided by application and perseverance, resolute will and purpose, and almost sublime patience,—borne up throughout by his passionate enthusiasm for discovery and research,—he succeeded in laying bare and digging up an amount of historical treasures, the like of which has probably never before been collected by the industry of any one man. Not less than two miles of bas-reliefs were thus brought to light by Mr. Layard. The selection of these valuable antiquities, now placed in the British Museum, was found so curiously corroborative of the scriptural records of events which occurred some three thousand years ago, that they burst upon the world almost like a new revelation. And the story of the disentombment of these remarkable works, as told by Mr. Layard himself in his 'Monuments of Nineveh,' will always be regarded as one of the most charming and unaffected records which we possess of individual enterprise, industry, and energy.

The career of the Comte de Buffon presents another remarkable illustration of the power of patient industry as well as of his own saying, that "Genius is patience." Notwithstanding the great results achieved by him in natural history, Buffon, when a youth, was regarded as of mediocre talents. His mind was slow in forming itself, and slow in reproducing what it had acquired. He was also constitutionally indolent; and being born to good estate, it might be supposed that he would indulge his liking for ease and luxury. Instead of which, he early formed the resolution of denying himself pleasure, and devoting himself to study and self-culture. Regarding time as a treasure that was limited, and finding that he was losing many hours by lying a-bed in the mornings, he determined to break himself of the habit. He struggled hard against it for some time, but failed in being able to rise at the hour he had fixed. He then called his servant, Joseph, to his help, and promised him the reward of a crown every time that he succeeded in getting him up before six. At first, when called, Buffon declined to rise—pleaded that he was ill, or pretended anger at being disturbed; and on the Count at length getting up, Joseph found that he had earned nothing but reproaches for having permitted his master to lie a-bed contrary to his express orders. At length the valet determined to earn his crown; and again and again he forced Buffon to rise, notwithstanding his entreaties, expostulations, and threats of immediate discharge from his service. One morning Buffon was unusually obstinate, and Joseph found it necessary to resort to the extreme measure of dashing a basin of ice-cold water under the bed-clothes, the effect of which was instantaneous. By the persistent use of such means, Buffon at length conquered his habit; and he was accustomed to say that he owed to Joseph three or four volumes of his Natural History.

For forty years of his life, Buffon worked every morning at his desk from nine till two, and again in the evening from five till nine. His diligence was so continuous and so regular that it became habitual. His biographer has said of him, "Work was his necessity; his studies were the charm of his life; and towards the last term of his glorious career he frequently said that he still hoped to be able to consecrate to them a few more years." He was a most conscientious worker, always studying to give the reader his best thoughts, expressed in the very best manner. He was never wearied with touching and retouching his compositions, so that his style may be pronounced almost perfect. He wrote the 'Epoques de la Nature' not fewer than eleven times before he was satisfied with it; although he had thought over the work about fifty years. He was a thorough man of business, most orderly in everything; and he was accustomed to say that genius without order lost three-fourths of its power. His great success as a writer was the result mainly of his painstaking labour and diligent application. "Buffon," observed Madame Necker, "strongly persuaded that genius is the result of a profound attention directed to a particular subject, said that he was thoroughly wearied out when composing his first writings, but compelled himself to return to them and go over them carefully again, even when he thought he had already brought them to a certain degree of perfection; and that at length he found pleasure instead of weariness in this long and elaborate correction." It ought also to be added that Buffon wrote and published all his great works while afflicted by one of the most painful diseases to which the human frame is subject.

Literary life affords abundant illustrations of the same power of perseverance; and perhaps no career is more instructive, viewed in this light, than that of Sir Walter Scott. His admirable working qualities were trained in a lawyer's office, where he pursued for many years a sort of drudgery scarcely above that of a copying clerk. His daily dull routine made his evenings, which were his own, all the more sweet; and he generally devoted them to reading and study. He himself attributed to his prosaic office discipline that habit of steady, sober diligence, in which mere literary men are so often found wanting. As a copying clerk he was allowed 3d. for every page containing a certain number of words; and he sometimes, by extra work, was able to copy as many as 120 pages in twenty-four hours, thus earning some 30s.; out of which he would occasionally purchase an odd volume, otherwise beyond his means.

During his after-life Scott was wont to pride himself upon being a man of business, and he averred, in contradiction to what he called the cant of sonneteers, that there was no necessary connection between genius and an aversion or contempt for the common duties of life. On the contrary, he was of opinion that to spend some fair portion of every day in any matter-of-fact occupation was good for the higher faculties themselves in the upshot. While afterwards acting as clerk to the Court of Session in Edinburgh, he performed his literary work chiefly before breakfast, attending the court during the day, where he authenticated registered deeds and writings of various kinds. On the whole, says Lockhart, "it forms one of the most remarkable features in his history, that throughout the most active period of his literary career, he must have devoted a large proportion of his hours, during half at least of every year, to the conscientious discharge of professional duties." It was a principle of action which he laid down for himself, that he must earn his living by business, and not by literature. On one occasion he said, "I determined that literature should be my staff, not my crutch, and that the profits of my literary labour, however convenient otherwise, should not, if I could help it, become necessary to my ordinary expenses."

His punctuality was one of the most carefully cultivated of his habits, otherwise it had not been possible for him to get through so enormous an amount of literary labour. He made it a rule to answer every letter received by him on the same day, except where inquiry and deliberation were requisite. Nothing else could have enabled him to keep abreast with the flood of communications that poured in upon him and sometimes put his good nature to the severest test. It was his practice to rise by five o'clock, and light his own fire. He shaved and dressed with deliberation, and was seated at his desk by six o'clock, with his papers arranged before him in the most accurate order, his works of reference marshalled round him on the floor, while at least one favourite dog lay watching his eye, outside the line of books. Thus by the time the family assembled for breakfast, between nine and ten, he had done enough—to use his own words—to break the neck of the day's work. But with all his diligent and indefatigable industry, and his immense knowledge, the result of many years' patient labour, Scott always spoke with the greatest diffidence of his own powers. On one occasion he said, "Throughout every part of my career I have felt pinched and hampered by my own ignorance."

Such is true wisdom and humility; for the more a man really knows, the less conceited he will be. The student at Trinity College who went up to his professor to take leave of him because he had "finished his education," was wisely rebuked by the professor's reply, "Indeed! I am only beginning mine." The superficial person who has obtained a smattering of many things, but knows nothing well, may pride himself upon his gifts; but the sage humbly confesses that "all he knows is, that he knows nothing," or like Newton, that he has been only engaged in picking shells by the sea shore, while the great ocean of truth lies all unexplored before him.

The lives of second-rate literary men furnish equally remarkable illustrations of the power of perseverance. The late John Britton, author of 'The Beauties of England and Wales,' and of many valuable architectural works, was born in a miserable cot in Kingston, Wiltshire. His father had been a baker and maltster, but was ruined in trade and became insane while Britton was yet a child. The boy received very little schooling, but a great deal of bad example, which happily did not corrupt him. He was early in life set to labour with an uncle, a tavern-keeper in Clerkenwell, under whom he bottled, corked, and binned wine for more than five years. His health failing him, his uncle turned him adrift in the world, with only two guineas, the fruits of his five years' service, in his pocket. During the next seven years of his life he endured many vicissitudes and hardships. Yet he says, in his autobiography, "in my poor and obscure lodgings, at eighteenpence a week, I indulged in study, and often read in bed during the winter evenings, because I could not afford a fire." Travelling on foot to Bath, he there obtained an engagement as a cellarman, but shortly after we find him back in the metropolis again almost penniless, shoeless, and shirtless. He succeeded, however, in obtaining employment as a cellarman at the London Tavern, where it was his duty to be in the cellar from seven in the morning until eleven at night. His health broke down under this confinement in the dark, added to the heavy work; and he then engaged himself, at fifteen shillings a week, to an attorney,—for he had been diligently cultivating the art of writing during the few spare minutes that he could call his own. While in this employment, he devoted his leisure principally to perambulating the bookstalls, where he read books by snatches which he could not buy, and thus picked up a good deal of odd knowledge. Then he shifted to another office, at the advanced wages of twenty shillings a week, still reading and studying. At twenty-eight he was able to write a book, which he published under the title of 'The Enterprising Adventures of Pizarro;' and from that time until his death, during a period of about fifty-five years, Britton was occupied in laborious literary occupation. The number of his published works is not fewer than eighty-seven; the most important being 'The Cathedral Antiquities of England,' in fourteen volumes, a truly magnificent work; itself the best monument of John Britton's indefatigable industry.

London, the landscape gardener, was a man of somewhat similar character, possessed of an extraordinary working power. The son of a farmer near Edinburgh, he was early inured to work. His skill in drawing plans and making sketches of scenery induced his father to train him for a landscape gardener. During his apprenticeship he sat up two whole nights every week to study; yet he worked harder during the day than any labourer. In the course of his night studies he learnt French, and before he was eighteen he translated a life of Abelard for an Encyclopædia. He was so eager to make progress in life, that when only twenty, while working as a gardener in England, he wrote down in his note-book, "I am now twenty years of age, and perhaps a third part of my life has passed away, and yet what have I done to benefit my fellow men?" an unusual reflection for a youth of only twenty. From French he proceeded to learn German, and rapidly mastered that language. Having taken a large farm, for the purpose of introducing Scotch improvements in the art of agriculture, he shortly succeeded in realising a considerable income. The continent being thrown open at the end of the war, he travelled abroad for the purpose of inquiring into the system of gardening and agriculture in other countries. He twice repeated his journeys, and the results were published in his Encyclopædias, which are among the most remarkable works of their kind,— distinguished for the immense mass of useful matter which they contain, collected by an amount of industry and labour which has rarely been equalled.

The career of Samuel Drew is not less remarkable than any of those which we have cited. His father was a hard-working labourer of the parish of St. Austell, in Cornwall. Though poor, he contrived to send his two sons to a penny-a-week school in the neighbourhood. Jabez, the elder, took delight in learning, and made great progress in his lessons; but Samuel, the younger, was a dunce, notoriously given to mischief and playing truant. When about eight years old he was put to manual labour, earning three-halfpence a day as a buddle-boy at a tin mine. At ten he was apprenticed to a shoemaker, and while in this employment he endured much hardship,—living, as he used to say, "like a toad under a harrow." He often thought of running away and becoming a pirate, or something of the sort, and he seems to have grown in recklessness as he grew in years. In robbing orchards he was usually a leader; and, as he grew older, he delighted to take part in any poaching or smuggling adventure. When about seventeen, before his apprenticeship was out, he ran away, intending to enter on board a man-of-war; but, sleeping in a hay-field at night cooled him a little, and he returned to his trade.

Drew next removed to the neighbourhood of Plymouth to work at his shoemaking business, and while at Cawsand he won a prize for cudgel-playing, in which he seems to have been an adept. While living there, he had nearly lost his life in a smuggling exploit which he had joined, partly induced by the love of adventure, and partly by the love of gain, for his regular wages were not more than eight shillings a-week. One night, notice was given throughout Crafthole, that a smuggler was off the coast, ready to land her cargo; on which the male population of the place—nearly all smugglers—made for the shore. One party remained on the rocks to make signals and dispose of the goods as they were landed; and another manned the boats, Drew being of the latter party. The night was intensely dark, and very little of the cargo had been landed, when the wind rose, with a heavy sea. The men in the boats, however, determined to persevere, and several trips were made between the smuggler, now standing farther out to sea, and the shore. One of the men in the boat in which Drew was, had his hat blown off by the wind, and in attempting to recover it, the boat was upset. Three of the men were immediately drowned; the others clung to the boat for a time, but finding it drifting out to sea, they took to swimming. They were two miles from land, and the night was intensely dark. After being about three hours in the water, Drew reached a rock near the shore, with one or two others, where he remained benumbed with cold till morning, when he and his companions were discovered and taken off, more dead than alive. A keg of brandy from the cargo just landed was brought, the head knocked in with a hatchet, and a bowlfull of the liquid presented to the survivors; and, shortly after, Drew was able to walk two miles through deep snow, to his lodgings.

This was a very unpromising beginning of a life; and yet this same Drew, scapegrace, orchard-robber, shoemaker, cudgel-player, and smuggler, outlived the recklessness of his youth and became distinguished as a minister of the Gospel and a writer of good books. Happily, before it was too late, the energy which characterised him was turned into a more healthy direction, and rendered him as eminent in usefulness as he had before been in wickedness. His father again took him back to St. Austell, and found employment for him as a journeyman shoemaker. Perhaps his recent escape from death had tended to make the young man serious, as we shortly find him attracted by the forcible preaching of Dr. Adam Clarke, a minister of the Wesleyan Methodists. His brother having died about the same time, the impression of seriousness was deepened; and thenceforward he was an altered man. He began anew the work of education, for he had almost forgotten how to read and write; and even after several years' practice, a friend compared his writing to the traces of a spider dipped in ink set to crawl upon paper. Speaking of himself, about that time, Drew afterwards said, "The more I read, the more I felt my own ignorance; and the more I felt my ignorance, the more invincible became my energy to surmount it. Every leisure moment was now employed in reading one thing or another. Having to support myself by manual labour, my time for reading was but little, and to overcome this disadvantage, my usual method was to place a book before me while at meat, and at every repast I read five or six pages." The perusal of Locke's 'Essay on the Understanding' gave the first metaphysical turn to his mind. "It awakened me from my stupor," said he, "and induced me to form a resolution to abandon the grovelling views which I had been accustomed to entertain."

Drew began business on his own account, with a capital of a few shillings; but his character for steadiness was such that a neighbouring miller offered him a loan, which was accepted, and, success attending his industry, the debt was repaid at the end of a year. He started with a determination to "owe no man anything," and he held to it in the midst of many privations. Often he went to bed supperless, to avoid rising in debt. His ambition was to achieve independence by industry and economy, and in this he gradually succeeded. In the midst of incessant labour, he sedulously strove to improve his mind, studying astronomy, history, and metaphysics. He was induced to pursue the latter study chiefly because it required fewer books to consult than either of the others. "It appeared to be a thorny path," he said, "but I determined, nevertheless, to enter, and accordingly began to tread it."

Added to his labours in shoemaking and metaphysics, Drew became a local preacher and a class leader. He took an eager interest in politics, and his shop became a favourite resort with the village politicians. And when they did not come to him, he went to them to talk over public affairs. This so encroached upon his time that he found it necessary sometimes to work until midnight to make up for the hours lost during the day. His political fervour become the talk of the village. While busy one night hammering away at a shoe-sole, a little boy, seeing a light in the shop, put his mouth to the keyhole of the door, and called out in a shrill pipe, "Shoemaker! shoe-maker! work by night and run about by day!" A friend, to whom Drew afterwards told the story, asked, "And did not you run after the boy, and strap him?" "No, no," was the reply; "had a pistol been fired off at my ear, I could not have been more dismayed or confounded. I dropped my work, and said to myself, 'True, true! but you shall never have that to say of me again.' To me that cry was as the voice of God, and it has been a word in season throughout my life. I learnt from it not to leave till to-morrow the work of to-day, or to idle when I ought to be working."

From that moment Drew dropped politics, and stuck to his work, reading and studying in his spare hours: but he never allowed the latter pursuit to interfere with his business, though it frequently broke in upon his rest. He married, and thought of emigrating to America; but he remained working on. His literary taste first took the direction of poetical composition; and from some of the fragments which have been preserved, it appears that his speculations as to the immateriality and immortality of the soul had their origin in these poetical musings. His study was the kitchen, where his wife's bellows served him for a desk; and he wrote amidst the cries and cradlings of his children. Paine's 'Age of Reason' having appeared about this time and excited much interest, he composed a pamphlet in refutation of its arguments, which was published. He used afterwards to say that it was the 'Age of Reason' that made him an author. Various pamphlets from his pen shortly appeared in rapid succession, and a few years later, while still working at shoemaking, he wrote and published his admirable 'Essay on the Immateriality and Immortality of the Human Soul,' which he sold for twenty pounds, a great sum in his estimation at the time. The book went through many editions, and is still prized.

Drew was in no wise puffed up by his success, as many young authors are, but, long after he had become celebrated as a writer, used to be seen sweeping the street before his door, or helping his apprentices to carry in the winter's coals. Nor could he, for some time, bring himself to regard literature as a profession to live by. His first care was, to secure an honest livelihood by his business, and to put into the "lottery of literary success," as he termed it, only the surplus of his time. At length, however, he devoted himself wholly to literature, more particularly in connection with the Wesleyan body; editing one of their magazines, and superintending the publication of several of their denominational works. He also wrote in the 'Eclectic Review,' and compiled and published a valuable history of his native county, Cornwall, with numerous other works. Towards the close of his career, he said of himself,—"Raised from one of the lowest stations in society, I have endeavoured through life to bring my family into a state of respectability, by honest industry, frugality, and a high regard for my moral character. Divine providence has smiled on my exertions, and crowned my wishes with success."

The late Joseph Hume pursued a very different career, but worked in an equally persevering spirit. He was a man of moderate parts, but of great industry and unimpeachable honesty of purpose. The motto of his life was "Perseverance," and well, he acted up to it. His father dying while he was a mere child, his mother opened a small shop in Montrose, and toiled hard to maintain her family and bring them up respectably. Joseph she put apprentice to a surgeon, and educated for the medical profession. Having got his diploma, he made several voyages to India as ship's surgeon, [115] and afterwards obtained a cadetship in the Company's service. None worked harder, or lived more temperately, than he did, and, securing the confidence of his superiors, who found him a capable man in the performance of his duty, they gradually promoted him to higher offices. In 1803 he was with the division of the army under General Powell, in the Mahratta war; and the interpreter having died, Hume, who had meanwhile studied and mastered the native languages, was appointed in his stead. He was next made chief of the medical staff. But as if this were not enough to occupy his full working power, he undertook in addition the offices of paymaster and post-master, and filled them satisfactorily. He also contracted to supply the commissariat, which he did with advantage to the army and profit to himself. After about ten years' unremitting labour, he returned to England with a competency; and one of his first acts was to make provision for the poorer members of his family.

But Joseph Hume was not a man to enjoy the fruits of his industry in idleness. Work and occupation had become necessary for his comfort and happiness. To make himself fully acquainted with the actual state of his own country, and the condition of the people, he visited every town in the kingdom which then enjoyed any degree of manufacturing celebrity. He afterwards travelled abroad for the purpose of obtaining a knowledge of foreign states. Returned to England, he entered Parliament in 1812, and continued a member of that assembly, with a short interruption, for a period of about thirty-four years. His first recorded speech was on the subject of public education, and throughout his long and honourable career he took an active and earnest interest in that and all other questions calculated to elevate and improve the condition of the people—criminal reform, savings-banks, free trade, economy and retrenchment, extended representation, and such like measures, all of which he indefatigably promoted. Whatever subject he undertook, he worked at with all his might. He was not a good speaker, but what he said was believed to proceed from the lips of an honest, single-minded, accurate man. If ridicule, as Shaftesbury says, be the test of truth, Joseph Hume stood the test well. No man was more laughed at, but there he stood perpetually, and literally, "at his post." He was usually beaten on a division, but the influence which he exercised was nevertheless felt, and many important financial improvements were effected by him even with the vote directly against him. The amount of hard work which he contrived to get through was something extraordinary. He rose at six, wrote letters and arranged his papers for parliament; then, after breakfast, he received persons on business, sometimes as many as twenty in a morning. The House rarely assembled without him, and though the debate might be prolonged to two or three o'clock in the morning, his name was seldom found absent from the division. In short, to perform the work which he did, extending over so long a period, in the face of so many Administrations, week after week, year after year,—to be outvoted, beaten, laughed at, standing on many occasions almost alone,—to persevere in the face of every discouragement, preserving his temper unruffled, never relaxing in his energy or his hope, and living to see the greater number of his measures adopted with acclamation, must be regarded as one of the most remarkable illustrations of the power of human perseverance that biography can exhibit.

Enterprise

C

allied with the qualities of self-reliance and energy is that characteristic quality which so much conduces to success in life, and is generally expressed by the word "enterprise." It is distinct from energy, inasmuch as it is constantly active in discovering new fields for energy to exert itself in. We are familiar with examples of men who have won fortunes or gained renown, not because they pursued better or wiser courses, but because of some originality in their aims and methods, by which they were enabled to command the attention of the busy world long enough to wrest from it the special object of their choice.

True enterprise is constantly on the alert to discover some new want of society, some fertile source of profit or honor, some unexplored field of business, and is ready to supply the one or to take advantage of the other. It is nearly an indispensable element in these days of fierce competition. Every avenue of business is crowded, and as soon as it is known that one party has made a success by one method there are scores of eager aspirants ready to try the successful plan, so that straightway it, too, ceases to be unique, and, in becoming common, loses the power it formerly possessed of compelling success. Hence the late-comers in the field are doomed to failure, while they may at the same time be the better fitted for the peculiar work in hand. What they should do is to aim at success by new plans and methods. Every one knows the enthusiastic glow that animates the whole being of him who feels the ardor of an explorer, who surmounts difficulties by new and, before, unthought-of expedients, who plans and projects enterprises that had previously escaped the active minds of his fellow men.

It is by virtue of this very enthusiasm that the man of enterprise, who is so ready to adopt new measures, plans, and projects, is enabled to carry into his business or profession an energy and inspiration which is totally lacking on the part of those who are followers. Hence the latter ofttimes fail of success which their talents might almost be said to have promised them. Therefore, those who enter the lists to win life's battles must expect, if they would reach their goal, to wage the fight not only by the old methods but by the new. To use only those tactics which are sanctioned by usage is to invite defeat. Throw open the windows of your mind to new ideas, and keep at least abreast of the times, and, if possible, ahead of them. Nothing is more fatal to self-advancement than a stupid conservatism or a servile imitation. The days when a man could get rich by plodding on without enterprise and without taxing his brains have gone by. Mere industry and economy are not enough; there must be intelligence and original thought.

Whatever your calling, inventiveness, adaptability, promptness of decision, must direct and utilize your force, and if you do not find markets you must make them. In business you need not know many books, but you must know your trade and men. You may be slow at logic, but you must dart at chances. You may stick to your groove in politics, but in your business you must switch into new tracks, and shape yourself to every exigency. We emphasize this matter because in no country is the red-tapist so out of place as here. Every calling is filled with bold, keen, subtle-witted men, fertile in expedients and devices, who are perpetually inventing new ways of buying cheaply, underselling, or attracting custom; and the man who sticks doggedly to the old-fashioned methods—who runs in a perpetual rut—will find himself outstripped in the race of life, if he is not stranded on the sands of popular indifference. Keep, then, your eyes open and your wits about you, and you may distance all competitors; but, if you ignore all new methods, you will find yourself like a lugger contending with an ocean steamer.

It is enterprise that oils the wheels of energy and industry. Industry gathers together, with a frugal hand, the means whereby we are enabled to develop our plans and purposes. Energy gives us force whereby we gather the courage to persevere in the lines decided on, bids us put on a bold mien and go forth to do valiant battle against opposing circumstances. But it is enterprise that suggests ways and means to overcome difficulties that threaten to overwhelm us. It is enterprise that bids us explore entirely new fields, discovering expedients that enable us to change what, by the force of circumstances, was fast becoming a failure into a glorious victory, bringing to us wealth, position, and fame. It is to enterprise that we are indebted for those rich discoveries in scientific fields by which we decipher the records of past ages, and unravel the secrets which nature surrounded with mystery, compelling them to serve us.

It was enterprise that harnessed steam, teaching it to do our bidding, and brought the lightning down from the heavens to carry our thoughts to the uttermost parts of the earth. It is the spirit of enterprise driving curious minds to work in new directions that has given us all those useful and curious inventions, which have done so much to make this nineteenth-century civilization to shine with so lustrous a light. In short, it is enterprise that lifts the man of but mediocre abilities and attainments into the foremost ranks of the successful ones.

Enterprise is an inheritance and not an acquisition. But it can at the same time be improved by cultivation, the same as bodily strength or any mental faculty. He who would excel as a swimmer must be often in the water, and the gymnast does not spare himself long and fatiguing exertions. So of an enterprising spirit. Some men seem born with an overflow of this, while others possess it in a slight degree only. But if any would be known as enterprising men, they must not hesitate to show by their every-day actions that they rely upon themselves in cases of emergency, and the greater the necessity the better means of surmounting it are constantly discovered. They must not hesitate to try plans because they are new; but if sober judgment can discover no objection to it, they must seize upon the very novelty of the plan as an inducement, and be only the more eager to put it to the test. There is no life so routine but that it constantly affords scope for the exercise of enterprising energy. The very fact that you are finding it routine and commonplace should at once set you to work to devise some new way to change this.

Do not stand sighing, wishing, and waiting, but go to work with an energy and perseverance that will set every obstacle in the way of your success flying like leaves before a whirlwind. A weak and irresolute way of doing business will shipwreck your plans as readily as effects follow causes. You may have ambition enough to wish yourself on the topmost round of the ladder of success; but if you have not the requisite energy to commence and enterprise enough to push ahead even when you know you are off the beaten track, you will always remain at the bottom, or at least on the lower rounds. Providence has hidden a charm in difficult undertakings which is appreciated only by those who dare to grapple with them. But this can only be true when you, by your own exertions and the strength of your own self-reliance and enterprise, have achieved the results. Nothing can be more distasteful than to see men of apparently good abilities waiting for some one to come and help them over difficulties.

Be your own helper. If a rock rises up before you, roll it along or climb over it. If you want money, earn it. If you want confidence, prove yourself worthy of it. Do not be content with doing what has been done; surpass it. Deserve success and it will come. The sun does not rise like a rocket or go down like a bullet fired from a gun; slowly and surely it makes its rounds, and never tires. It is as easy to be a lead horse as a wheel horse. If the job be long, the pay will be greater; if the task be hard, the more competent you must be to do it. We must apportion our strength and exertions to the requisite tasks and duties. He who weakly shrinks from the struggle, who will offer no resistance, who will endure no labor nor fatigue, can neither fulfill his own vocation, nor contribute aught to the general welfare of mankind.

The spirit of the times demands that all who would rise in life shrink not back from labor, but it also demands that they exert themselves understandingly; that they spare no effort to master all the intricacies of the business or vocation in which they are engaged; that they be alert to discover new ways by which they may reach the desired goal easier than the old; that they bear in mind that sticking to the old ruts is only the right policy so long as no better way presents itself, and when that way is discovered, be not at all slow to improve it. If you do not, others more enterprising will rush forward to reap the profits it promises, and you will be left behind in the race. No matter what your position in life may be or the conditions which hem you in, there will be a "tide" in your affairs, "which, taken at its flood, leads on to fortune." But you must be ready to accept the chance. While you are hesitating and deliberating the occasion goes by, in most cases never to return again. Therefore, be prompt to seize it as it flies. Cultivate as far as possible the spirit of enterprise, for on that in a great degree depends your success or failure.

MGVT

MGVT
The store for the
IDEAL MAN
& WOMAN
www.mgvt.co.uk

www.ingramcontent.com/pod-product-compliance
Lightning Source LLC
Chambersburg PA
CBHW051310220526
45468CB00004B/1286